Picture book of

SUMMER

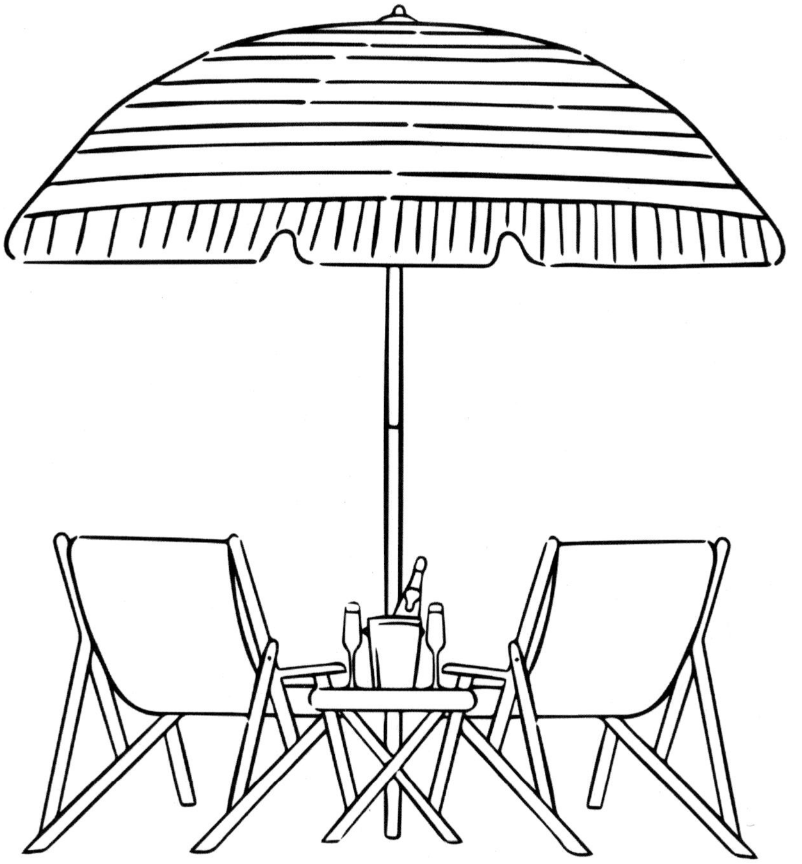

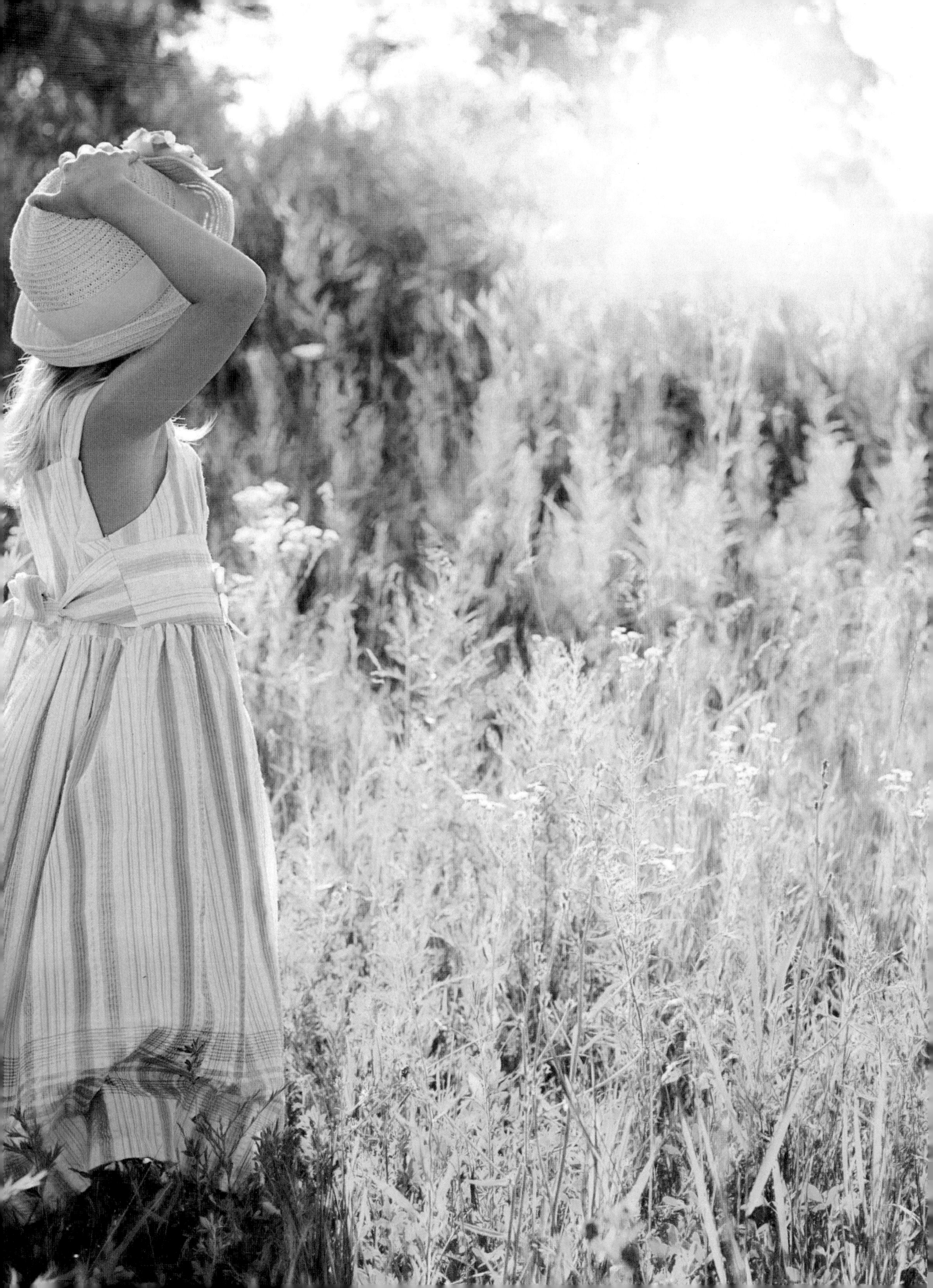

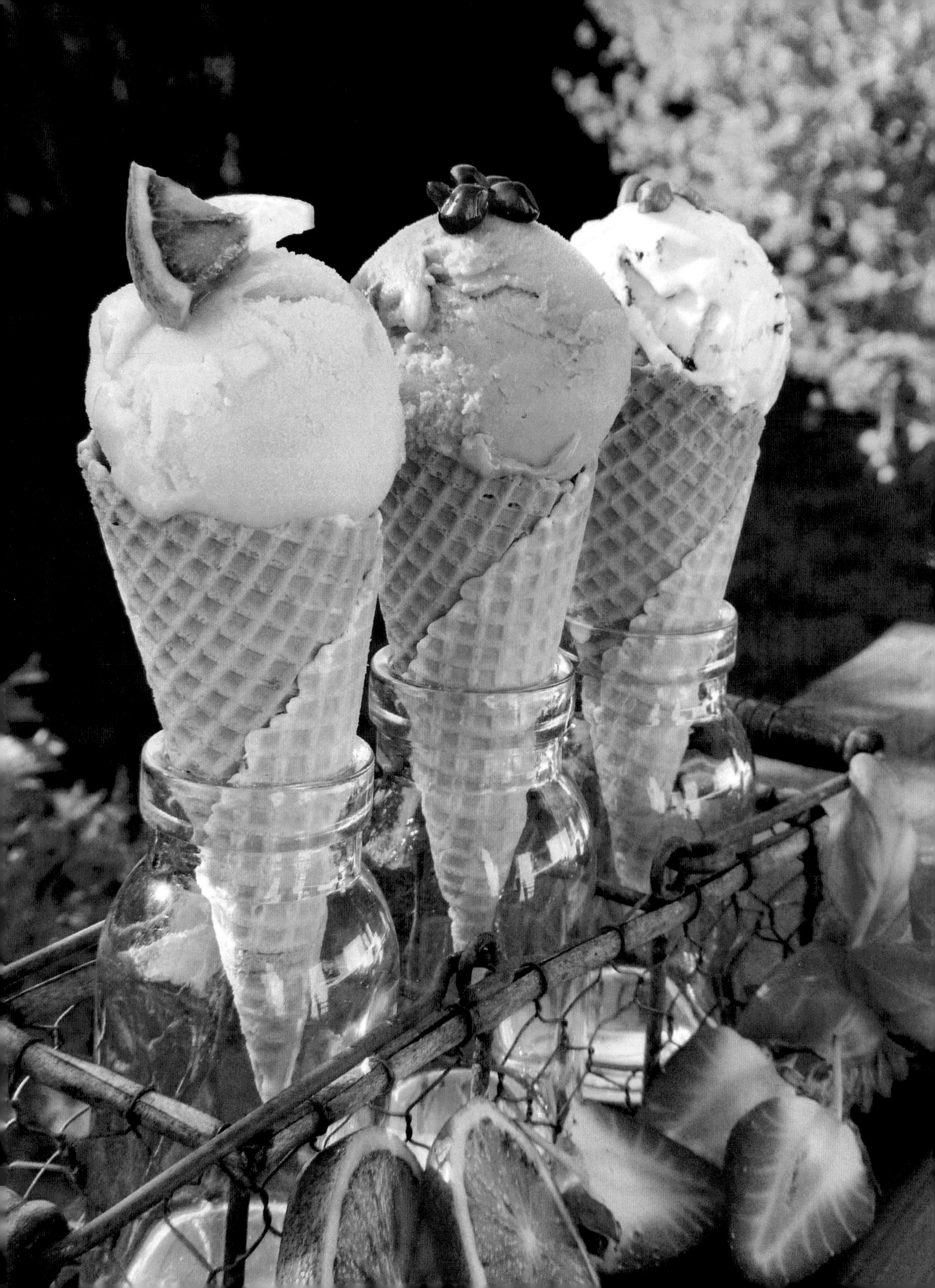

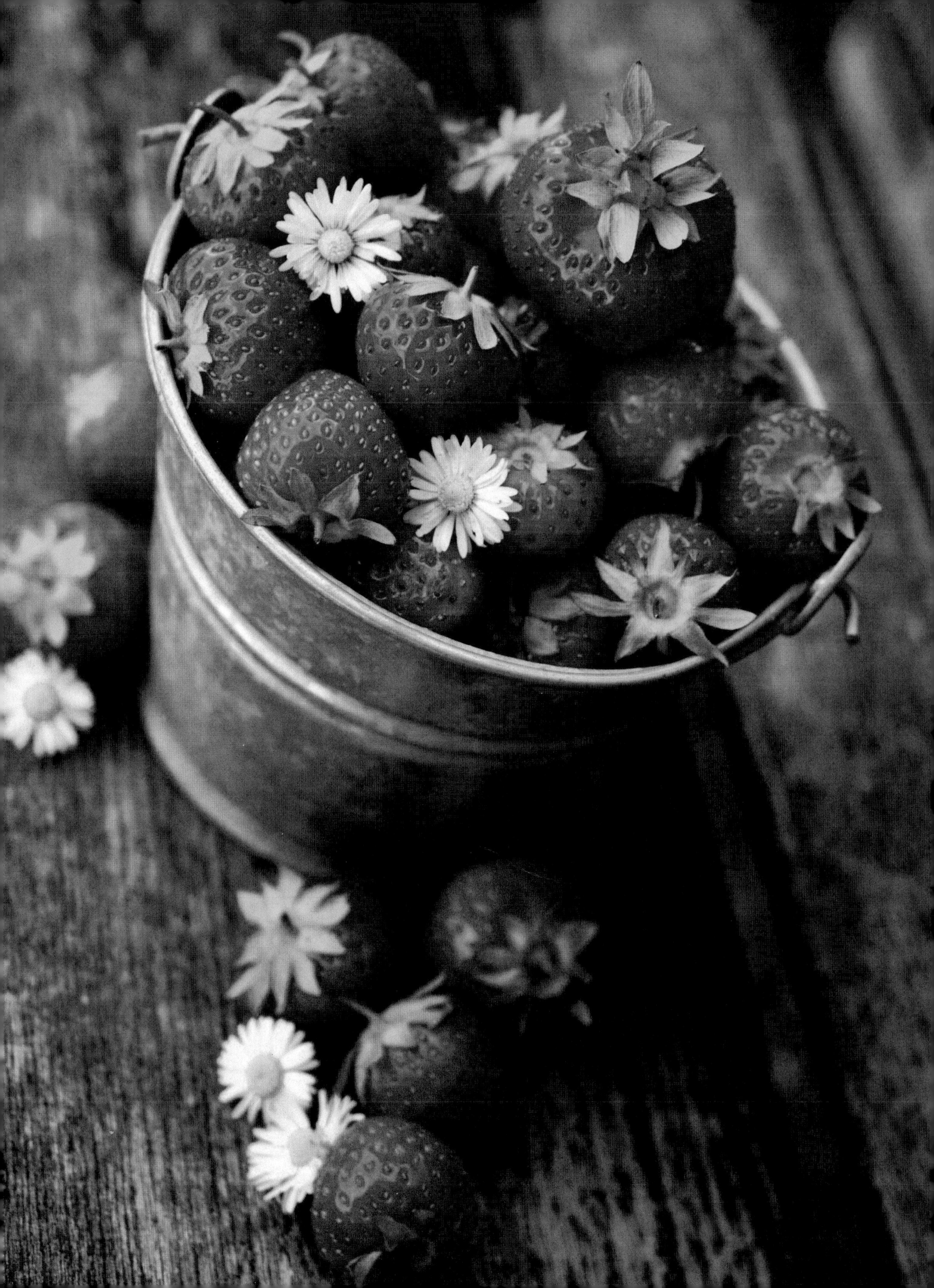

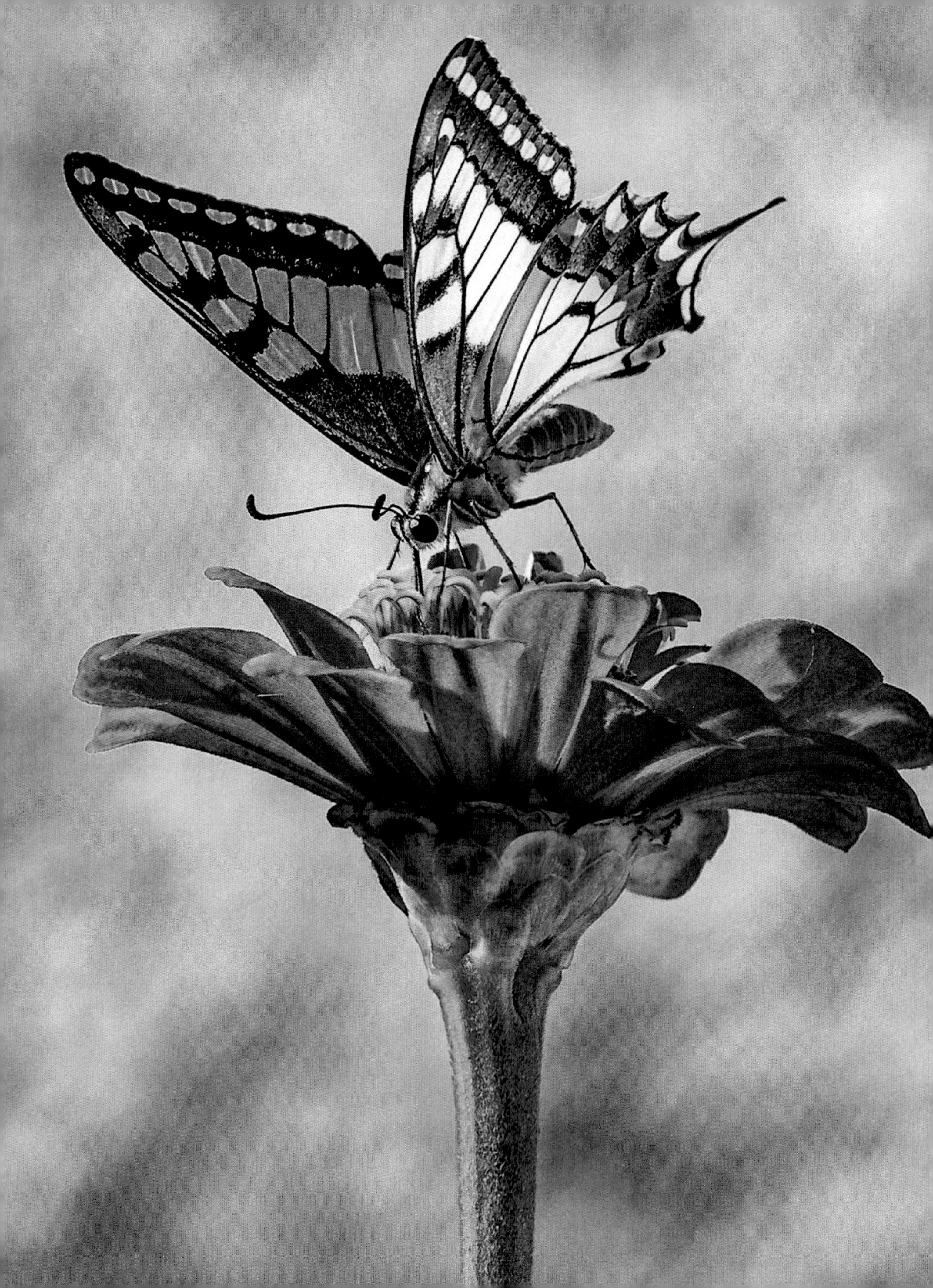

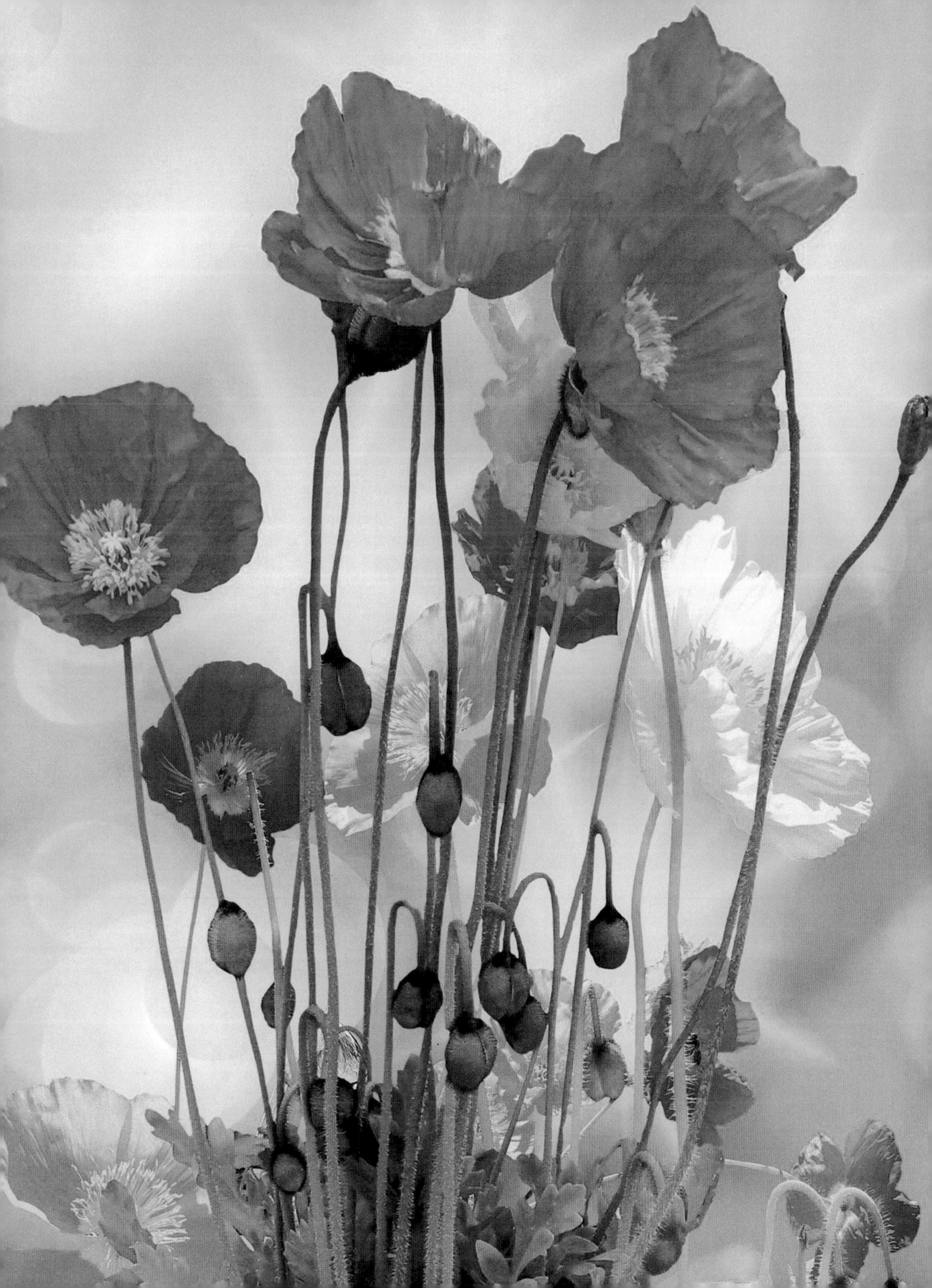

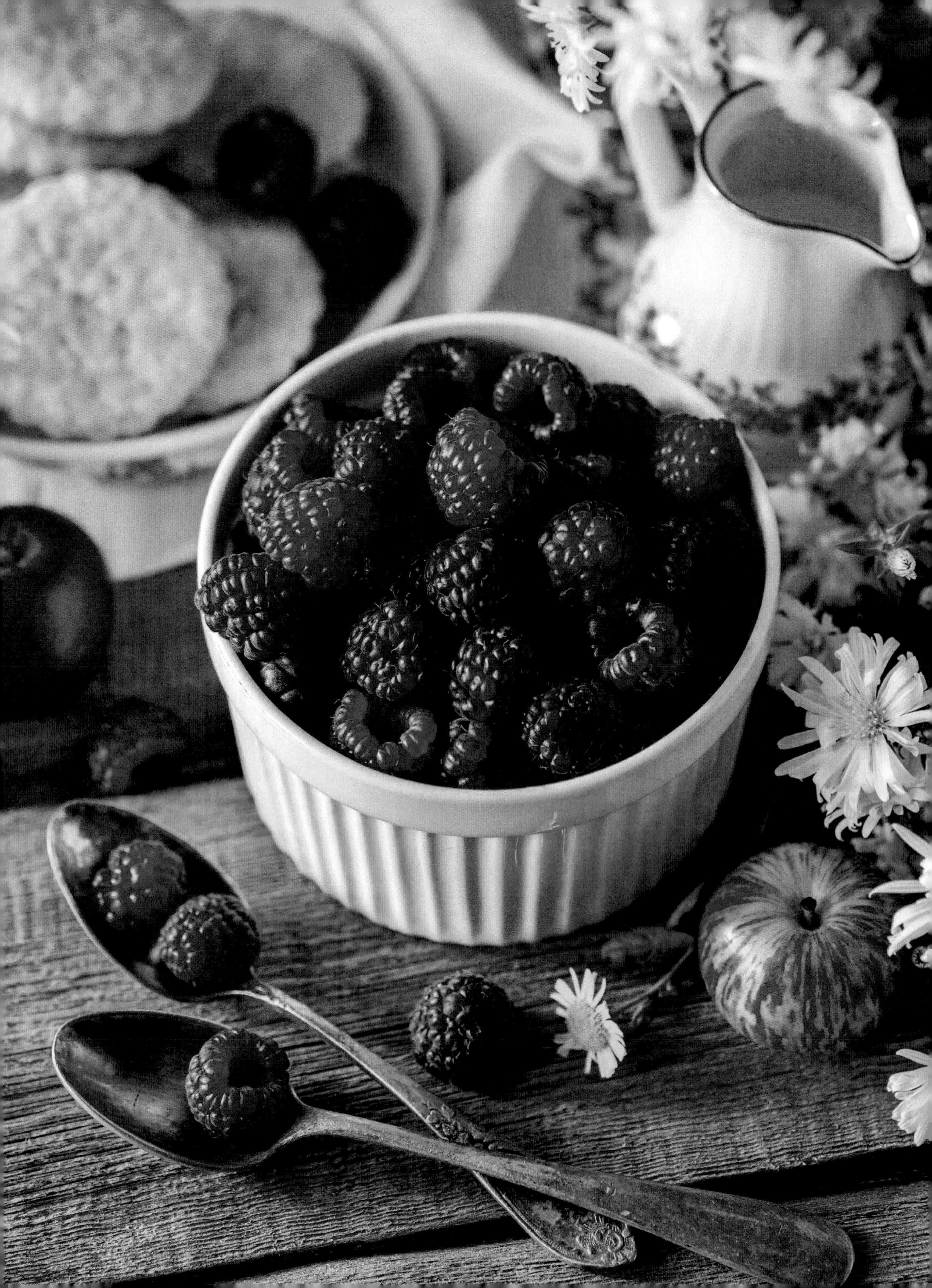

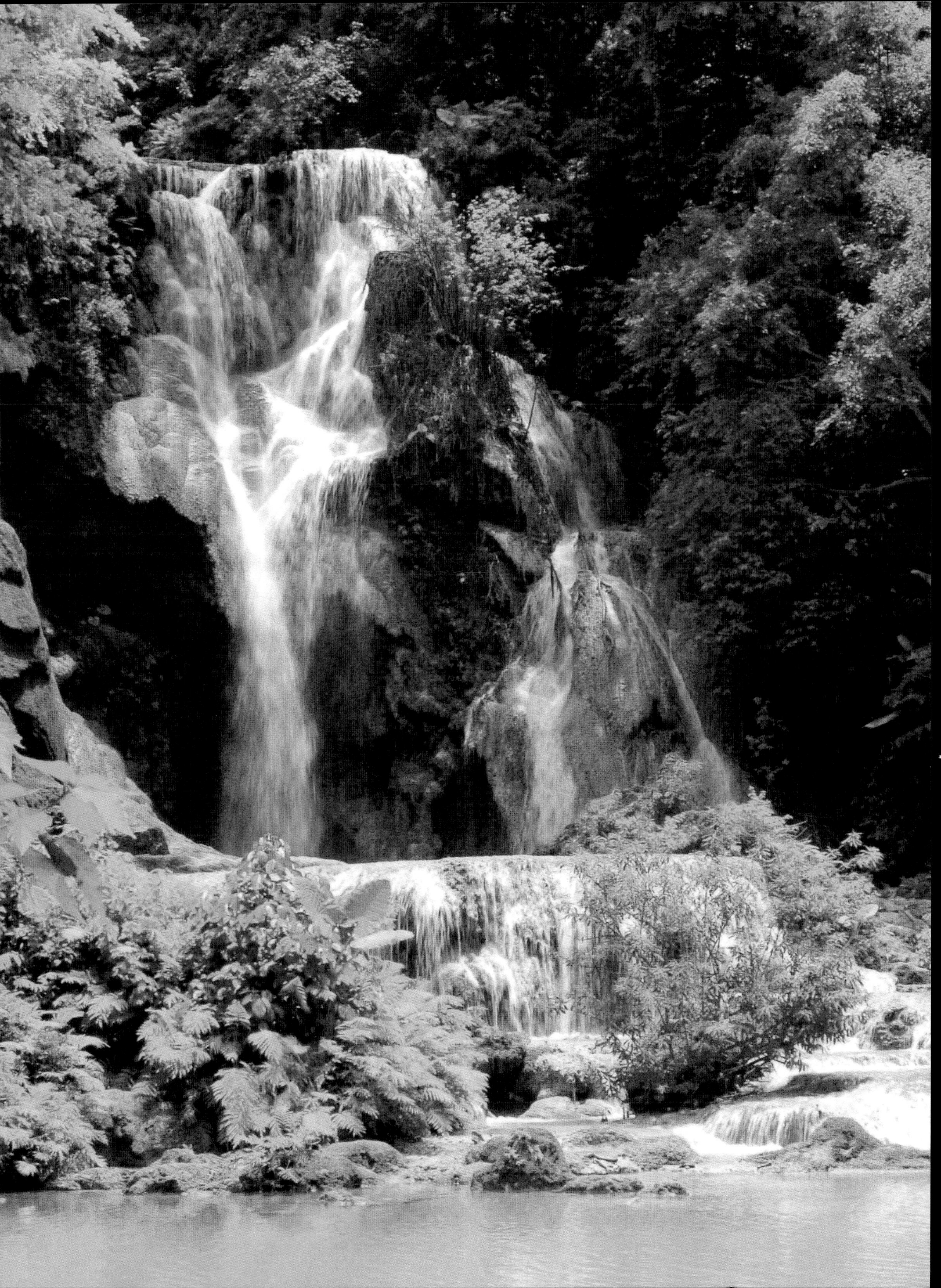

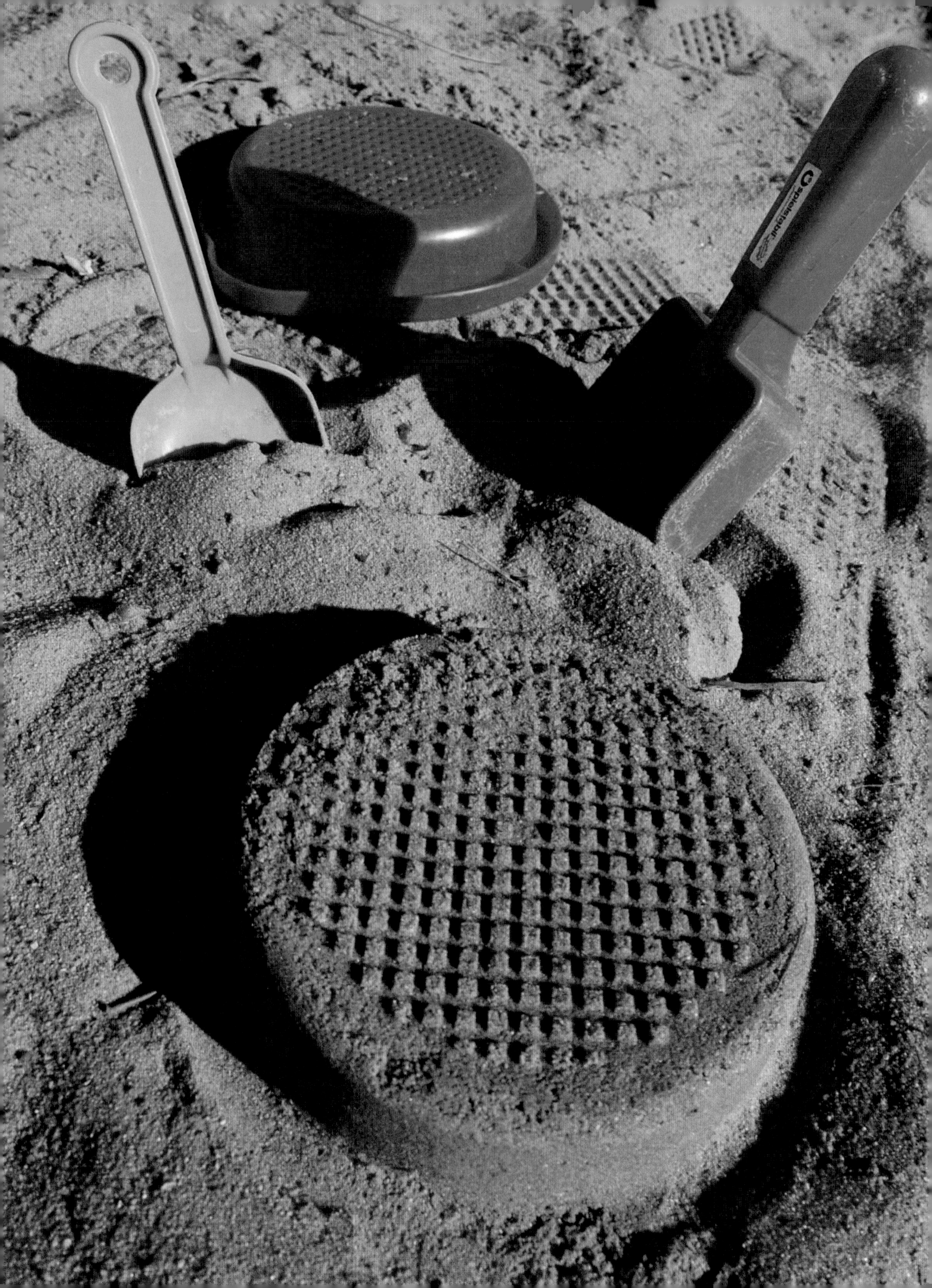
spielstabil

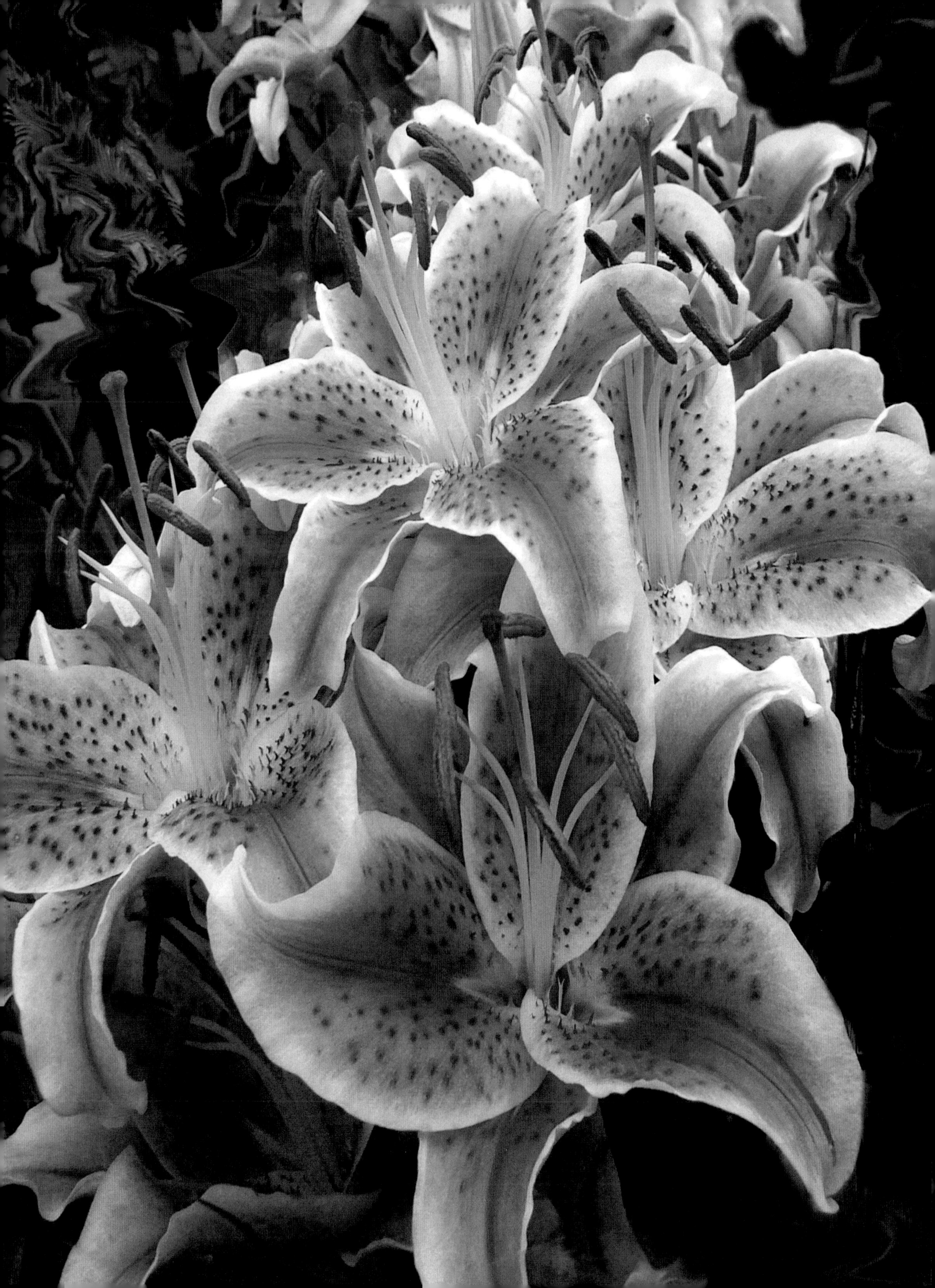

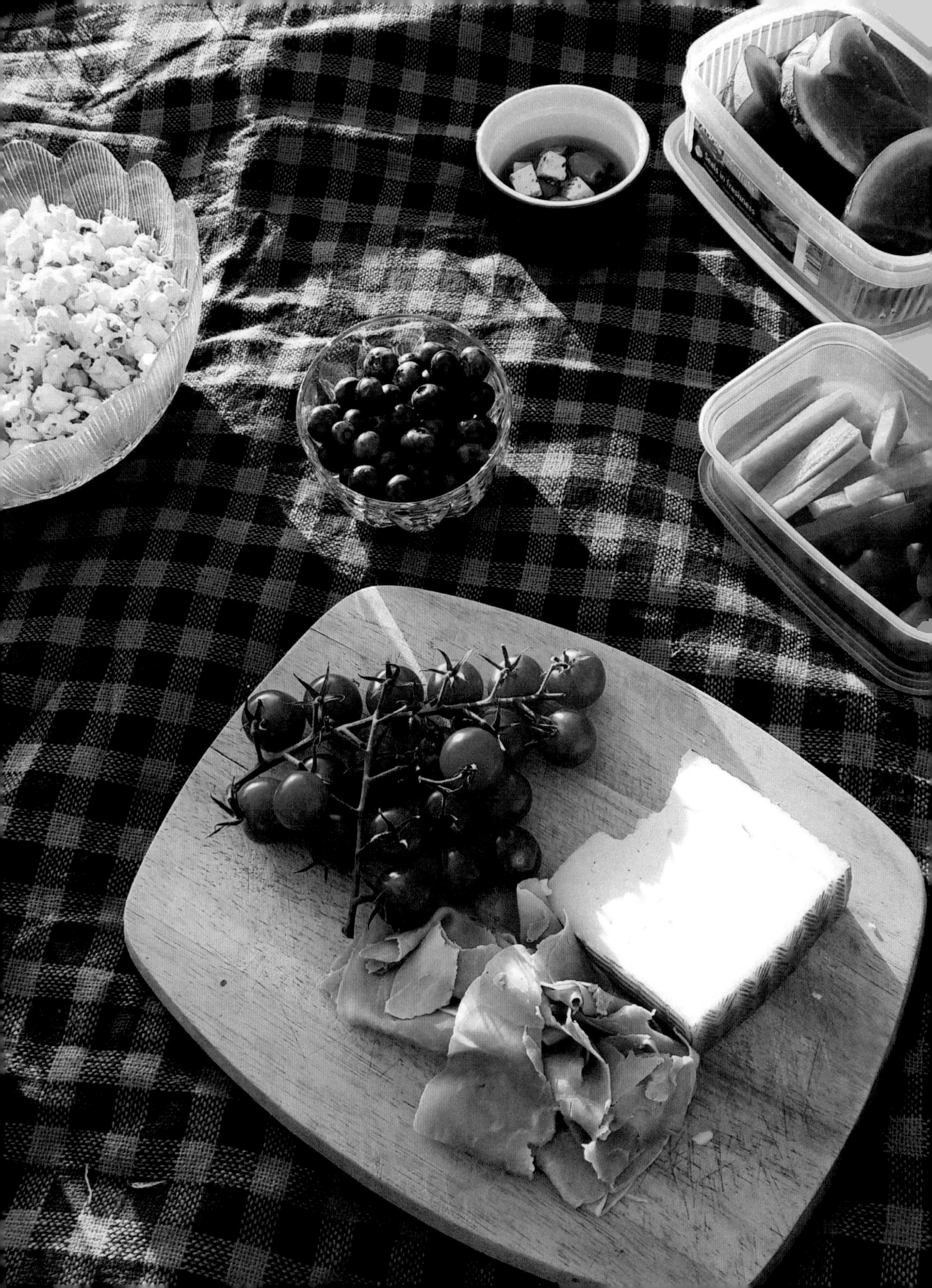
Seals in freshness

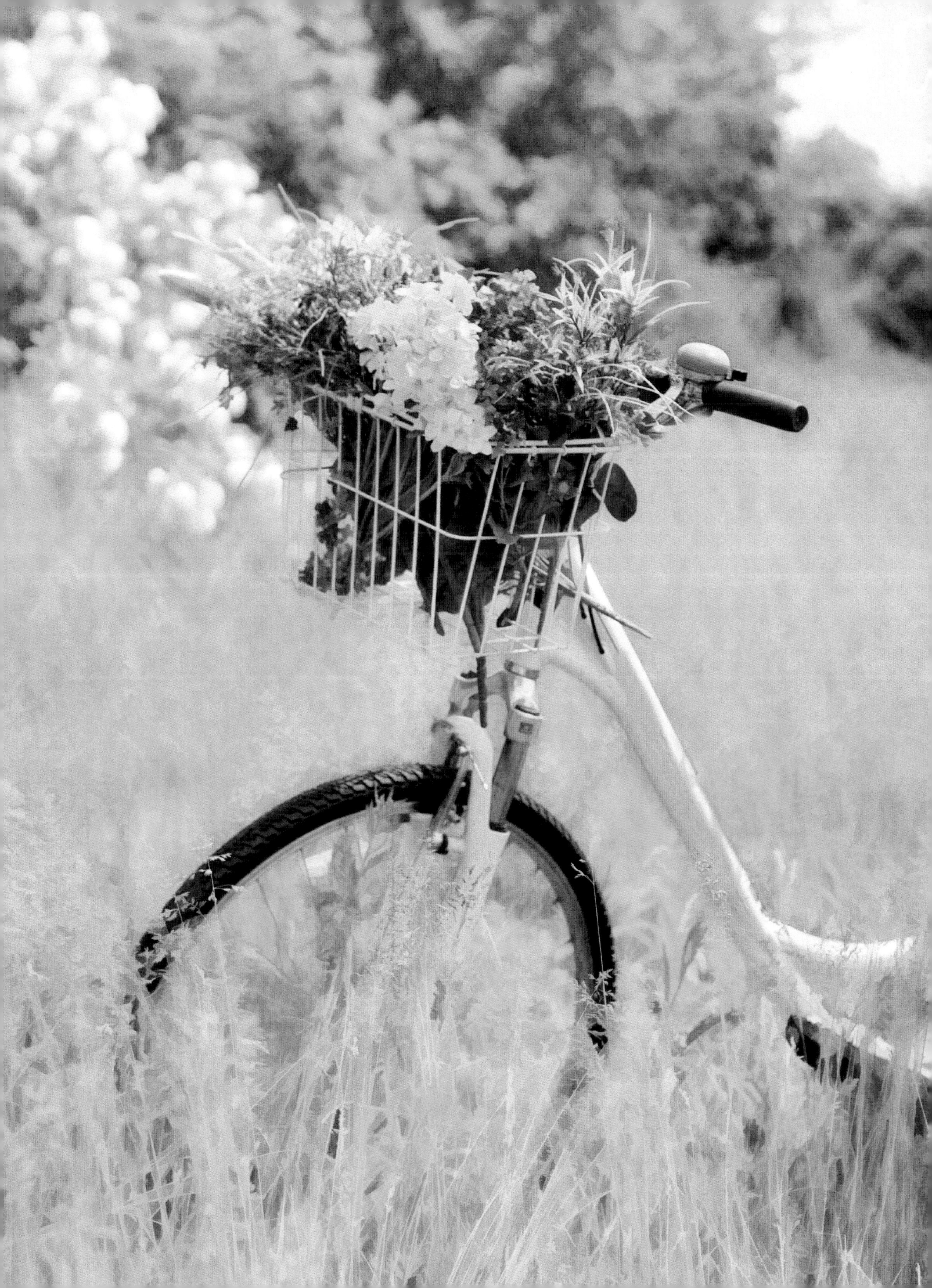

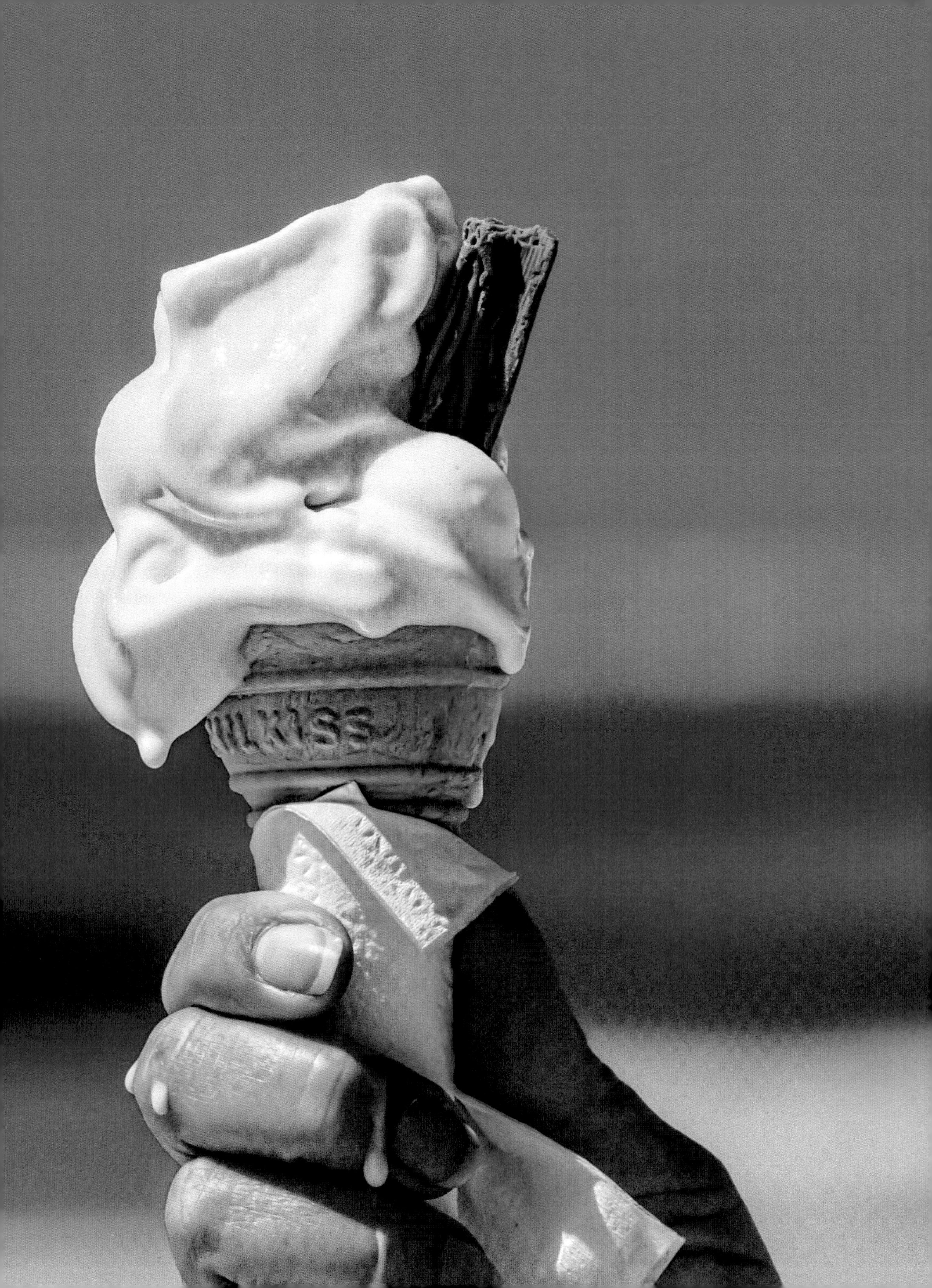

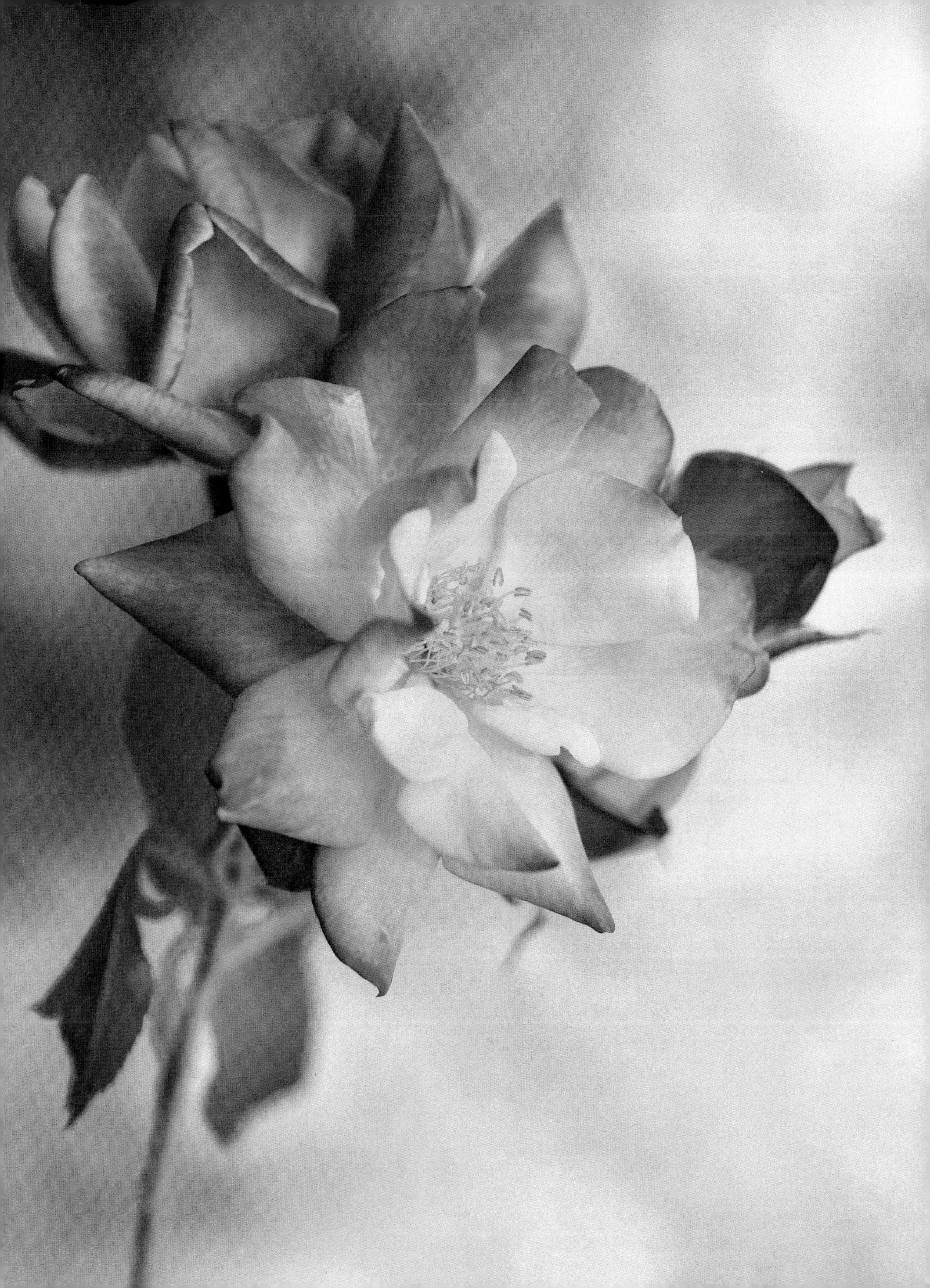

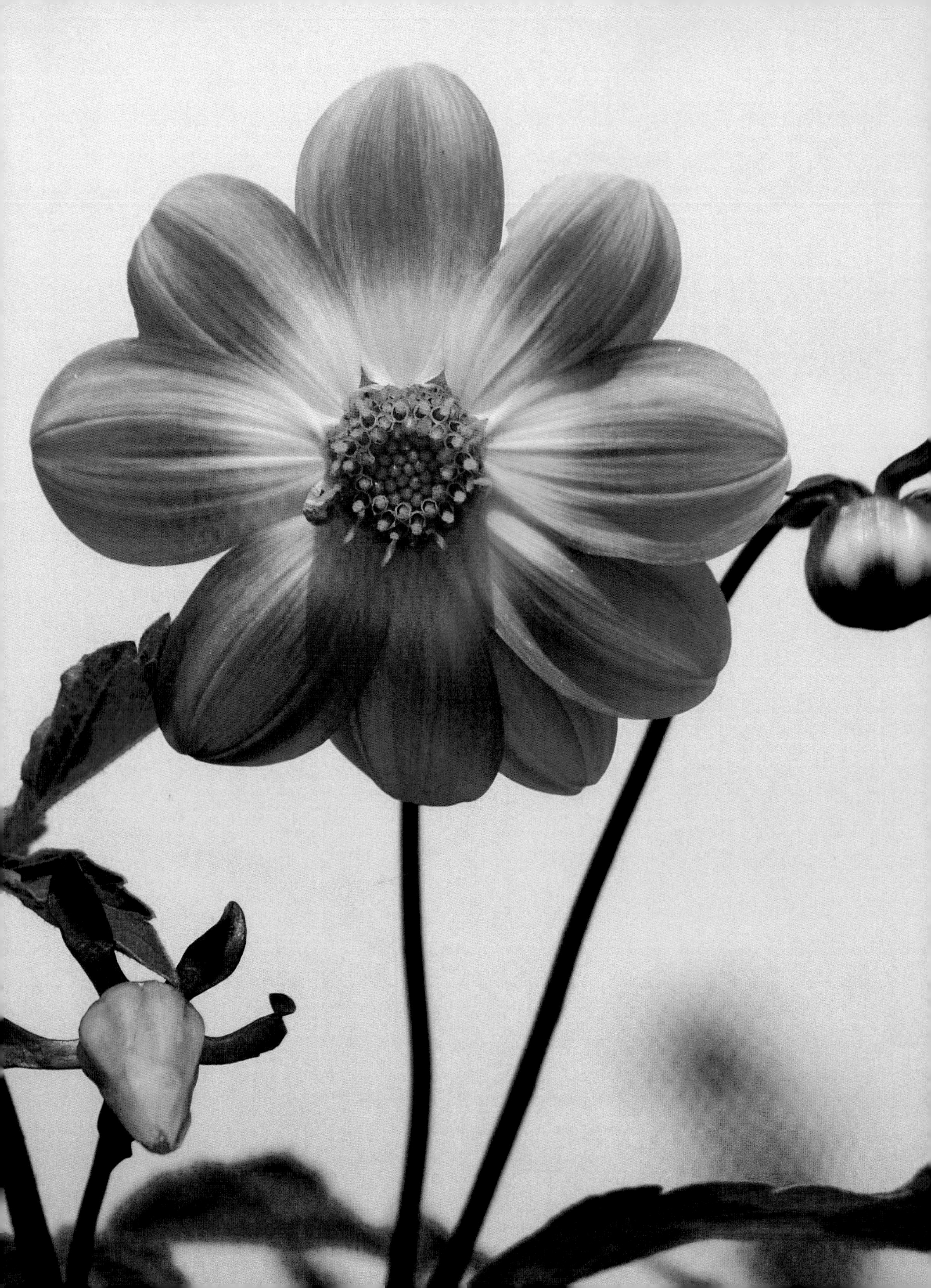

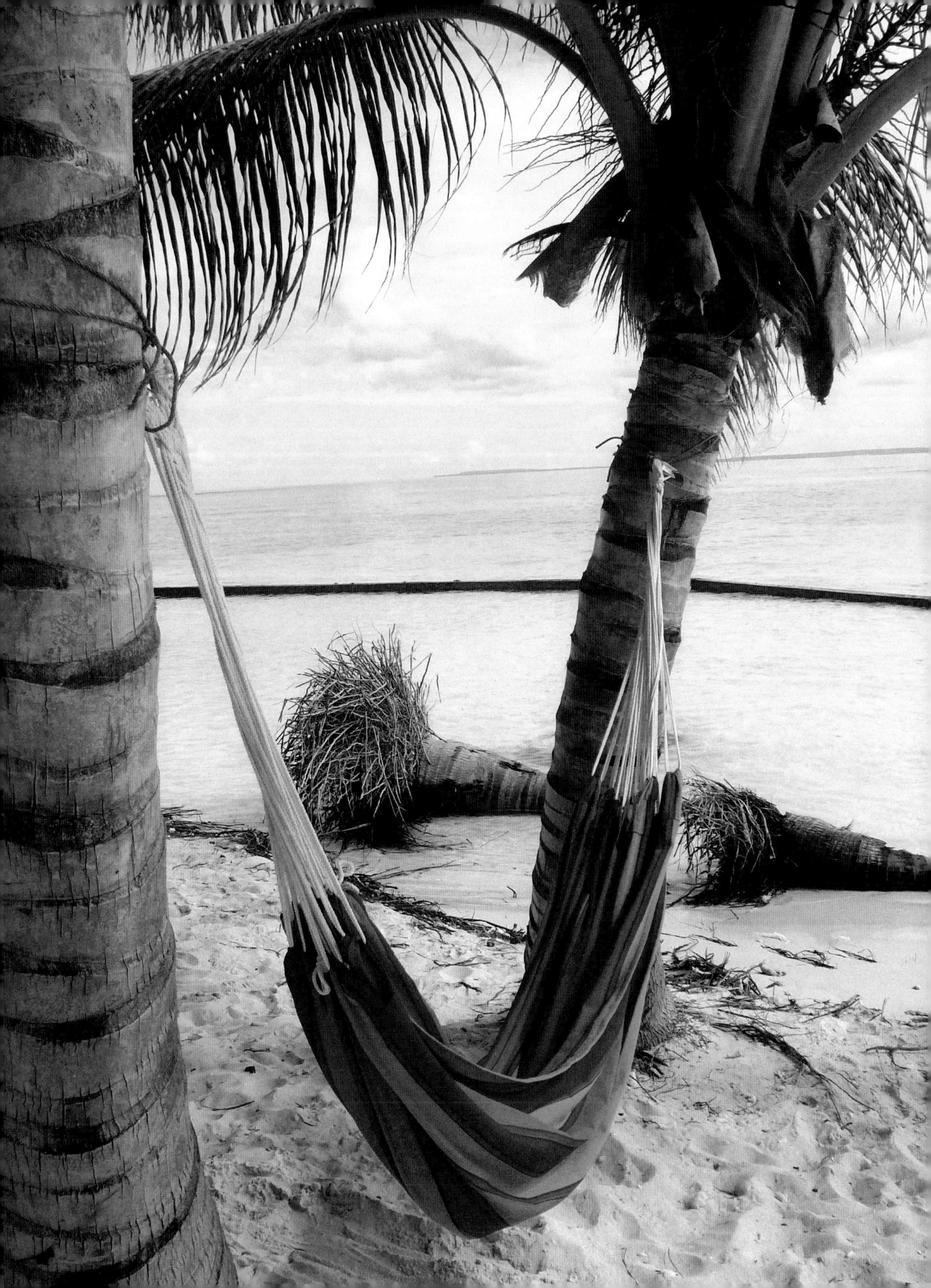

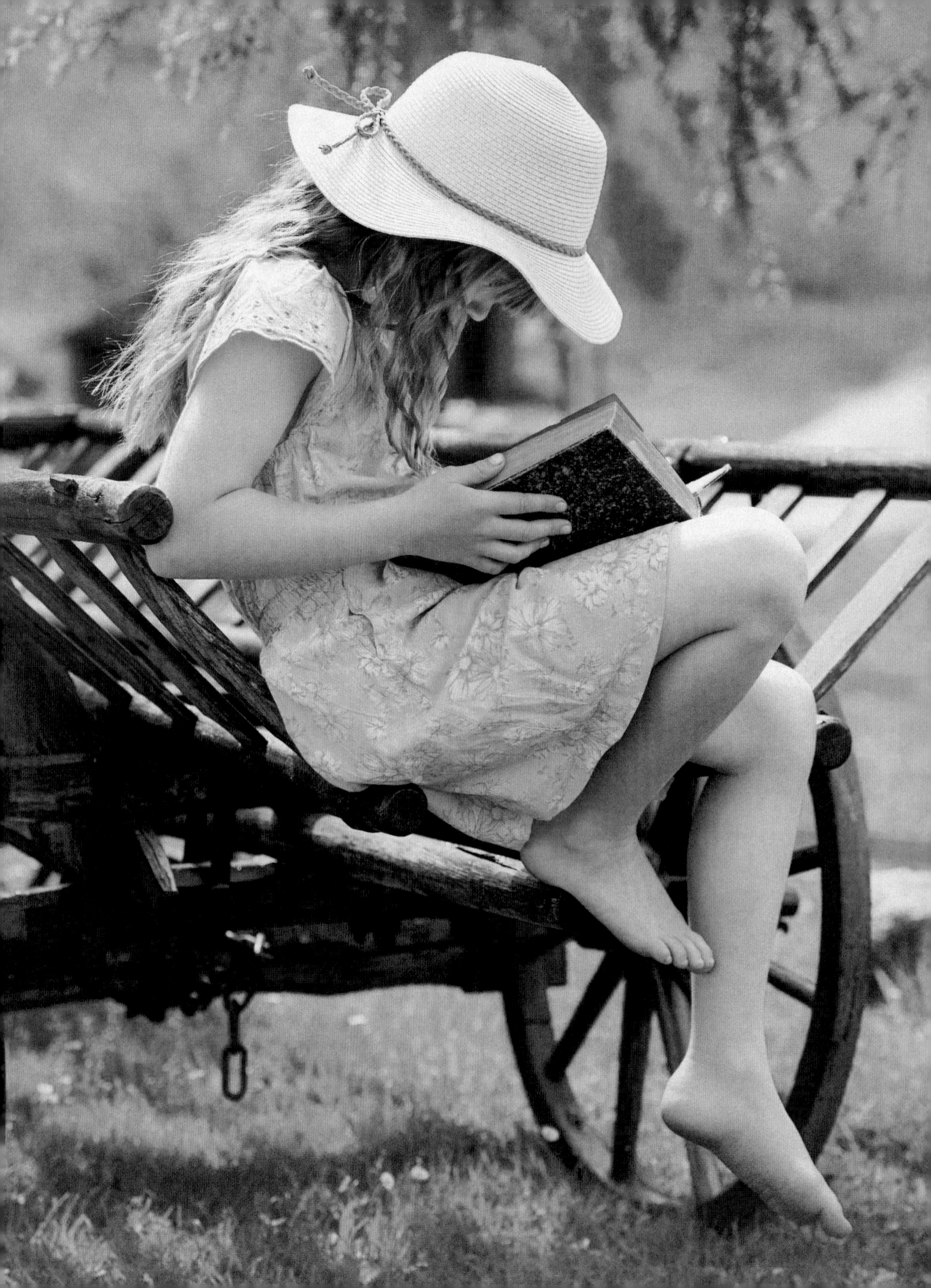

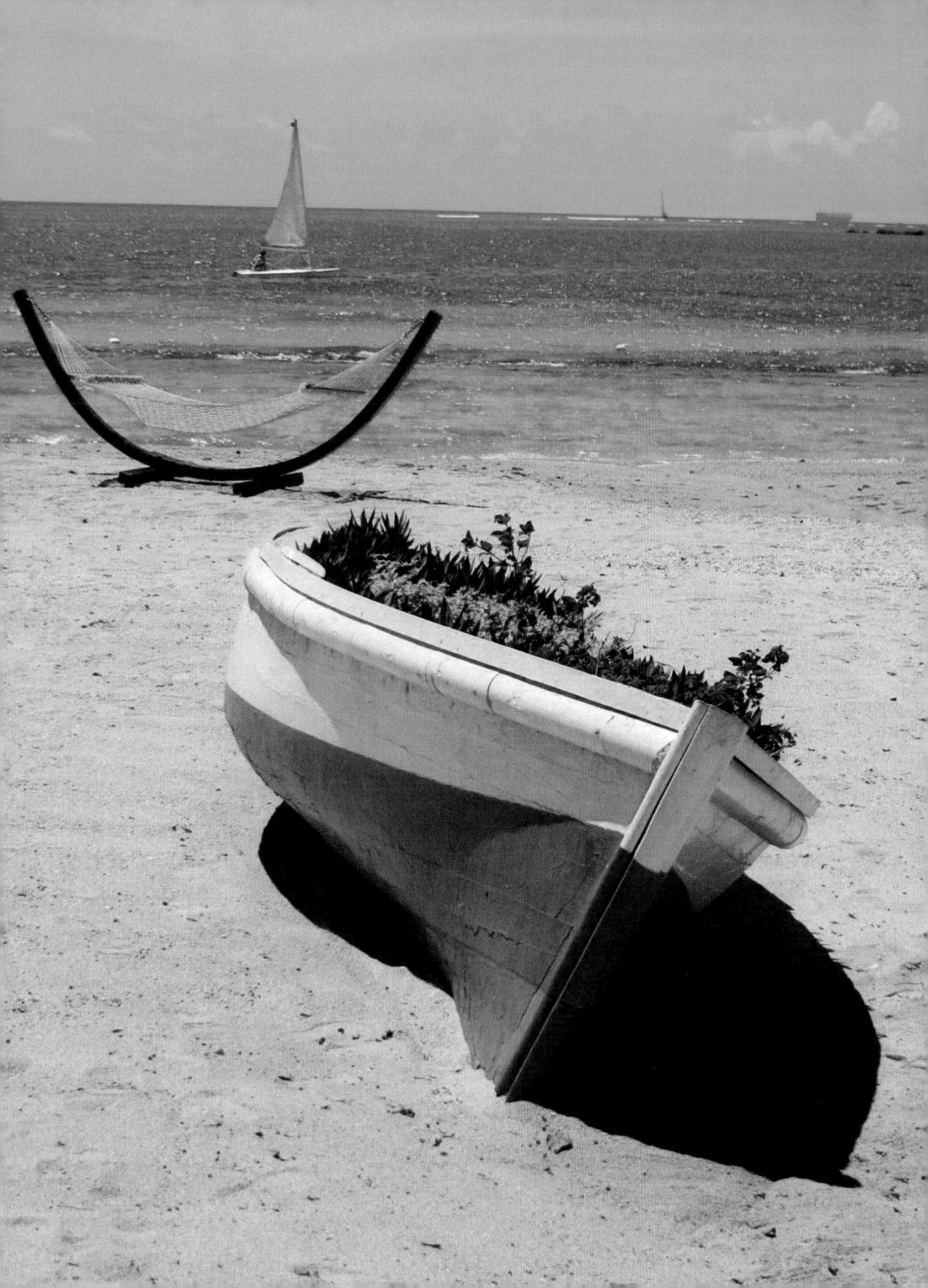

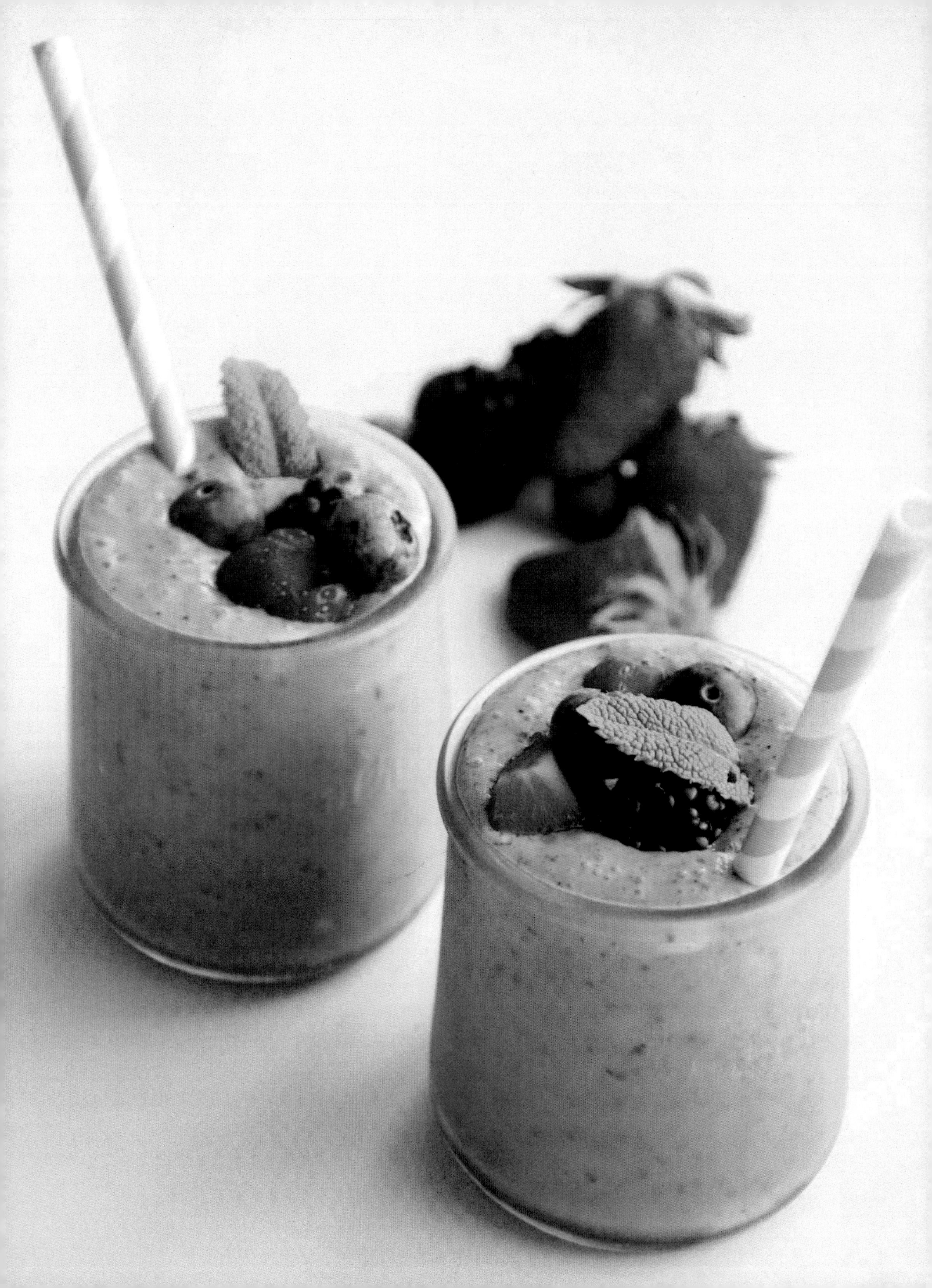

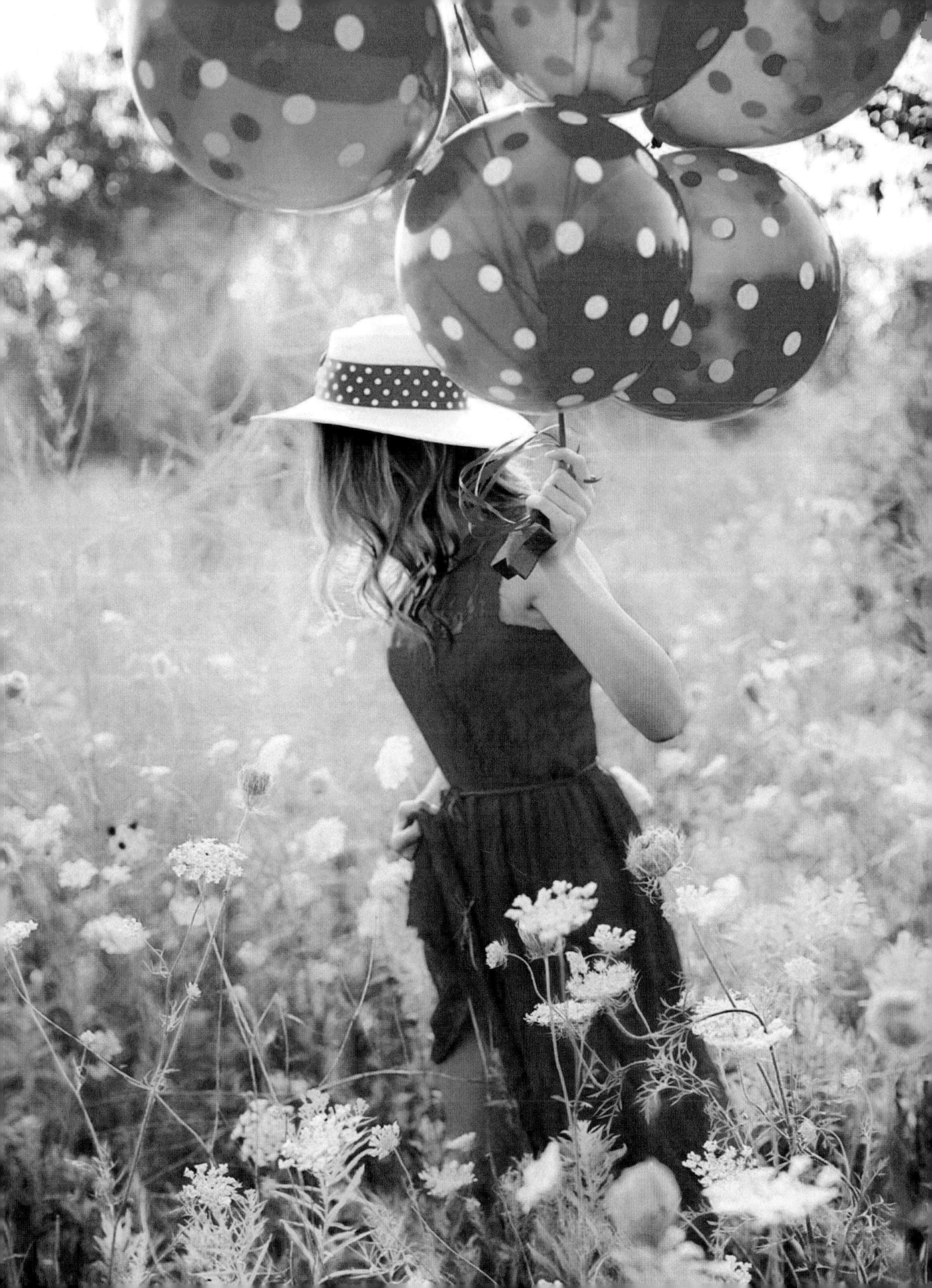

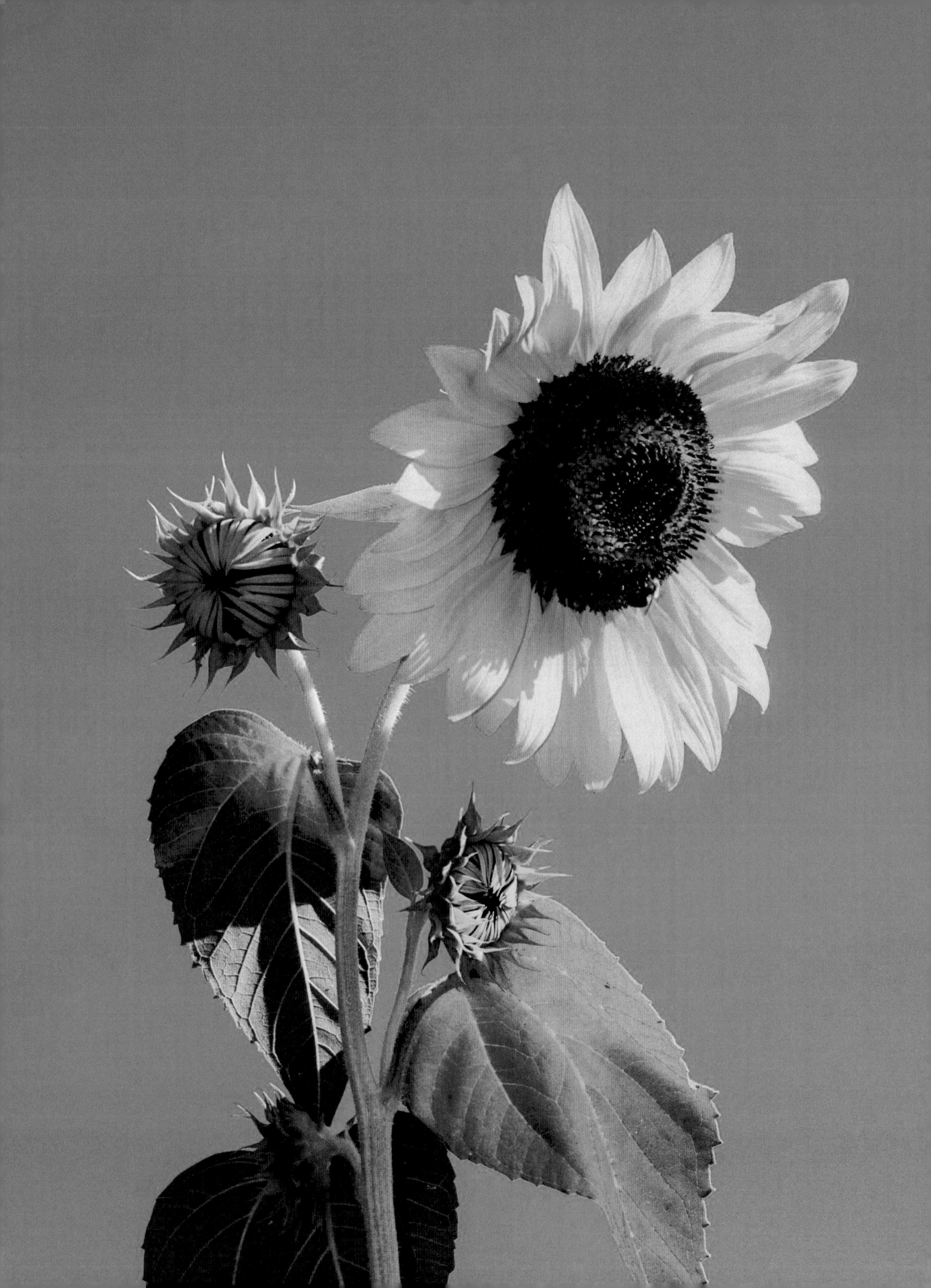

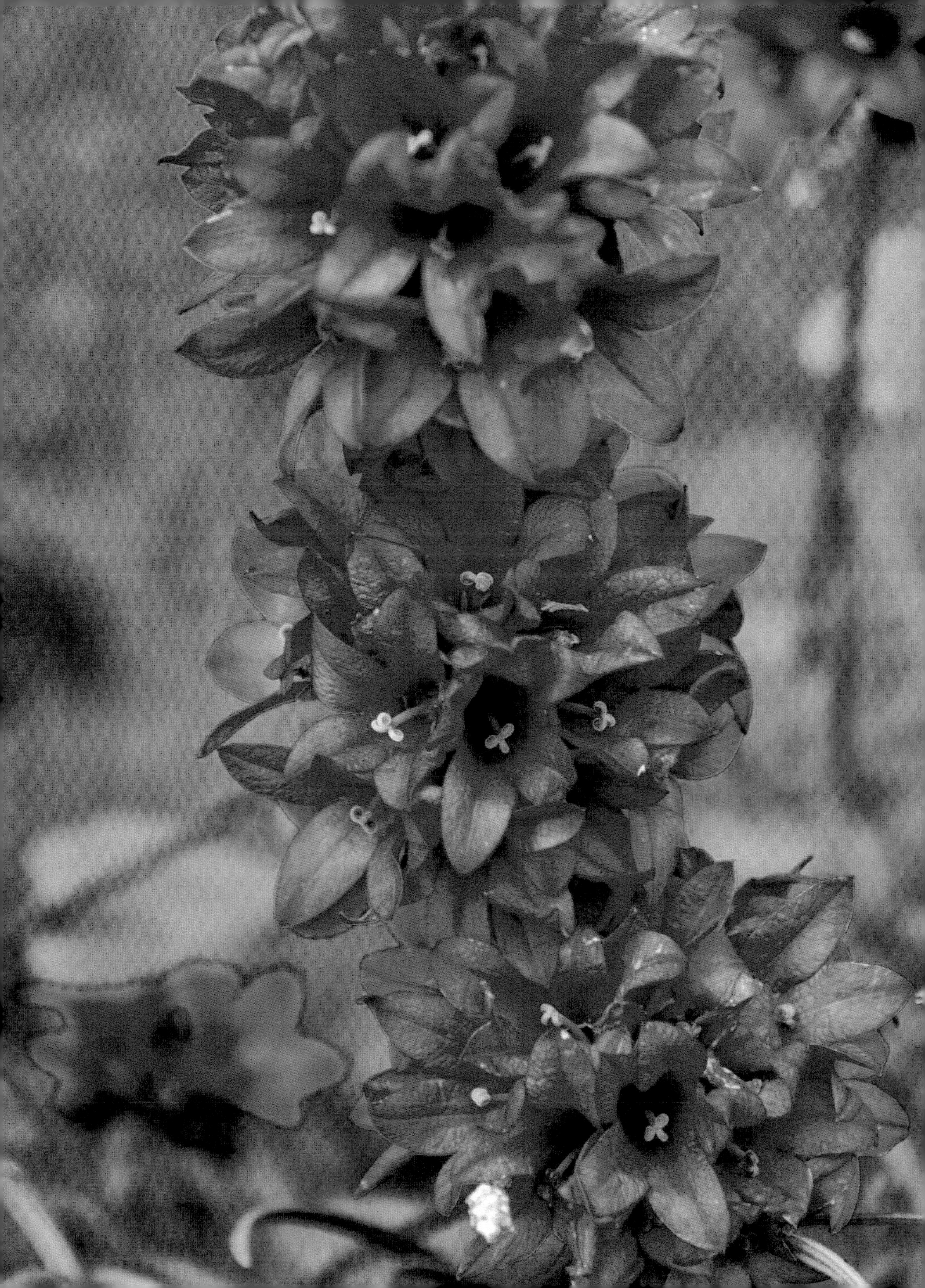

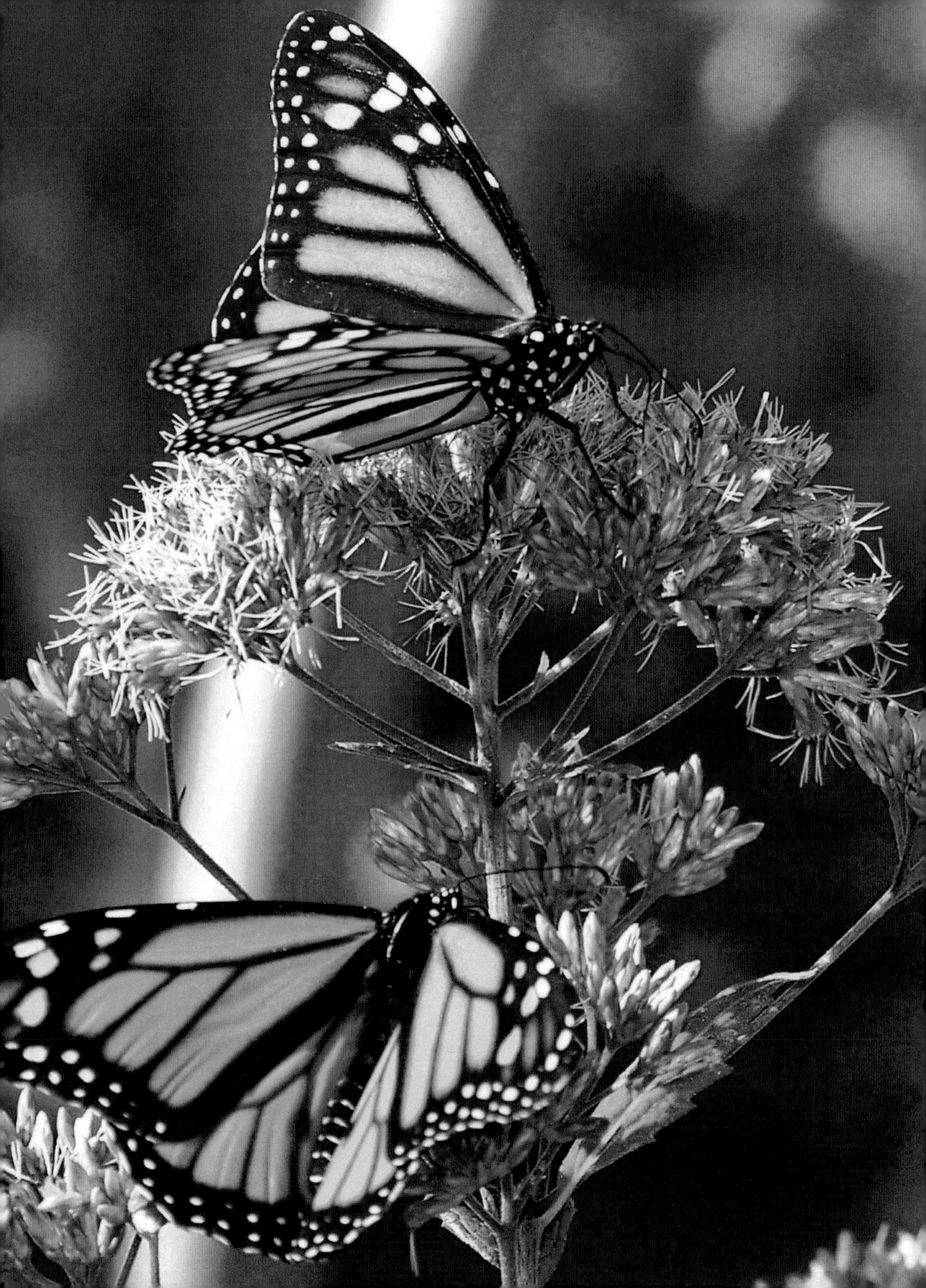

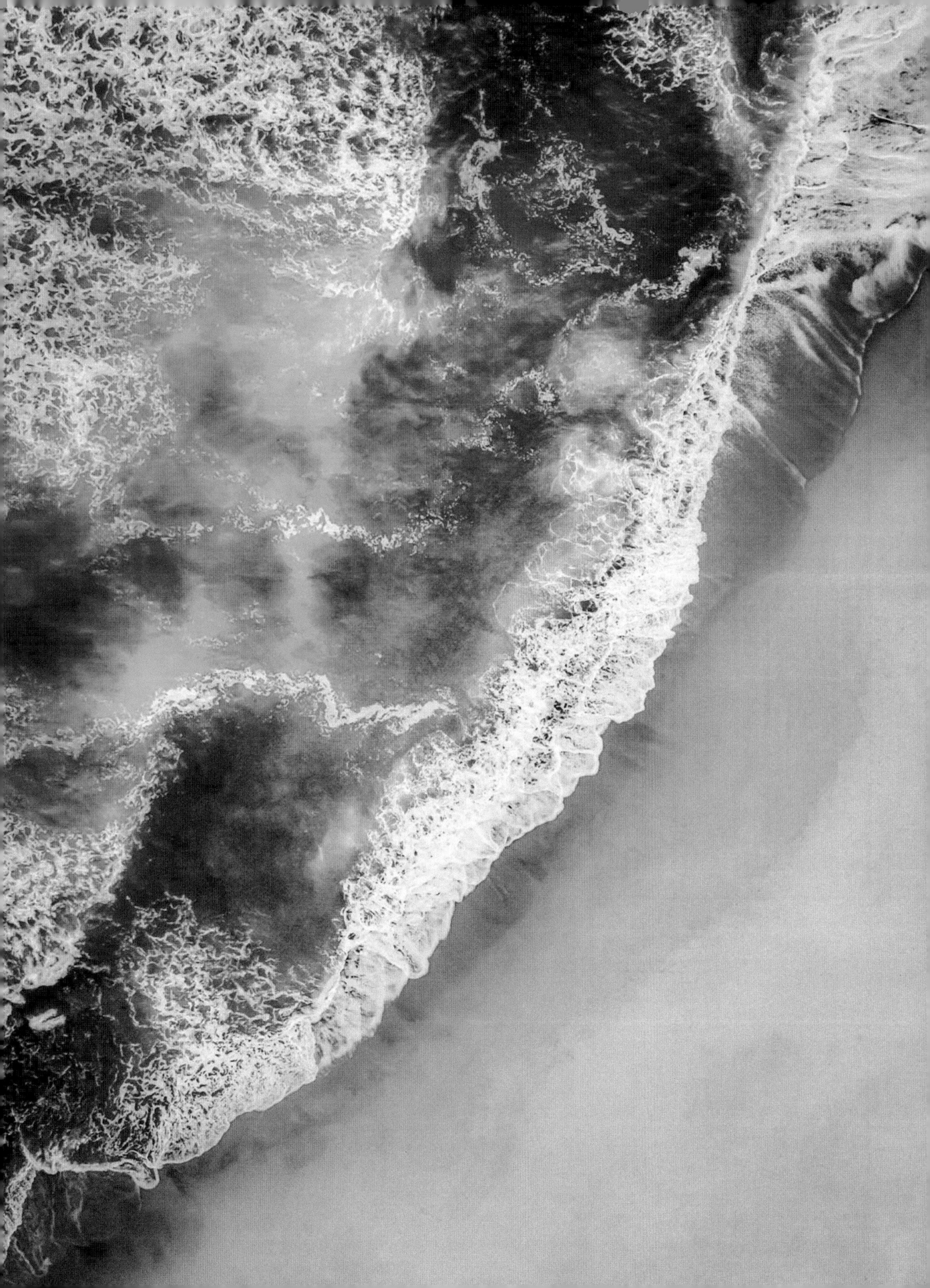

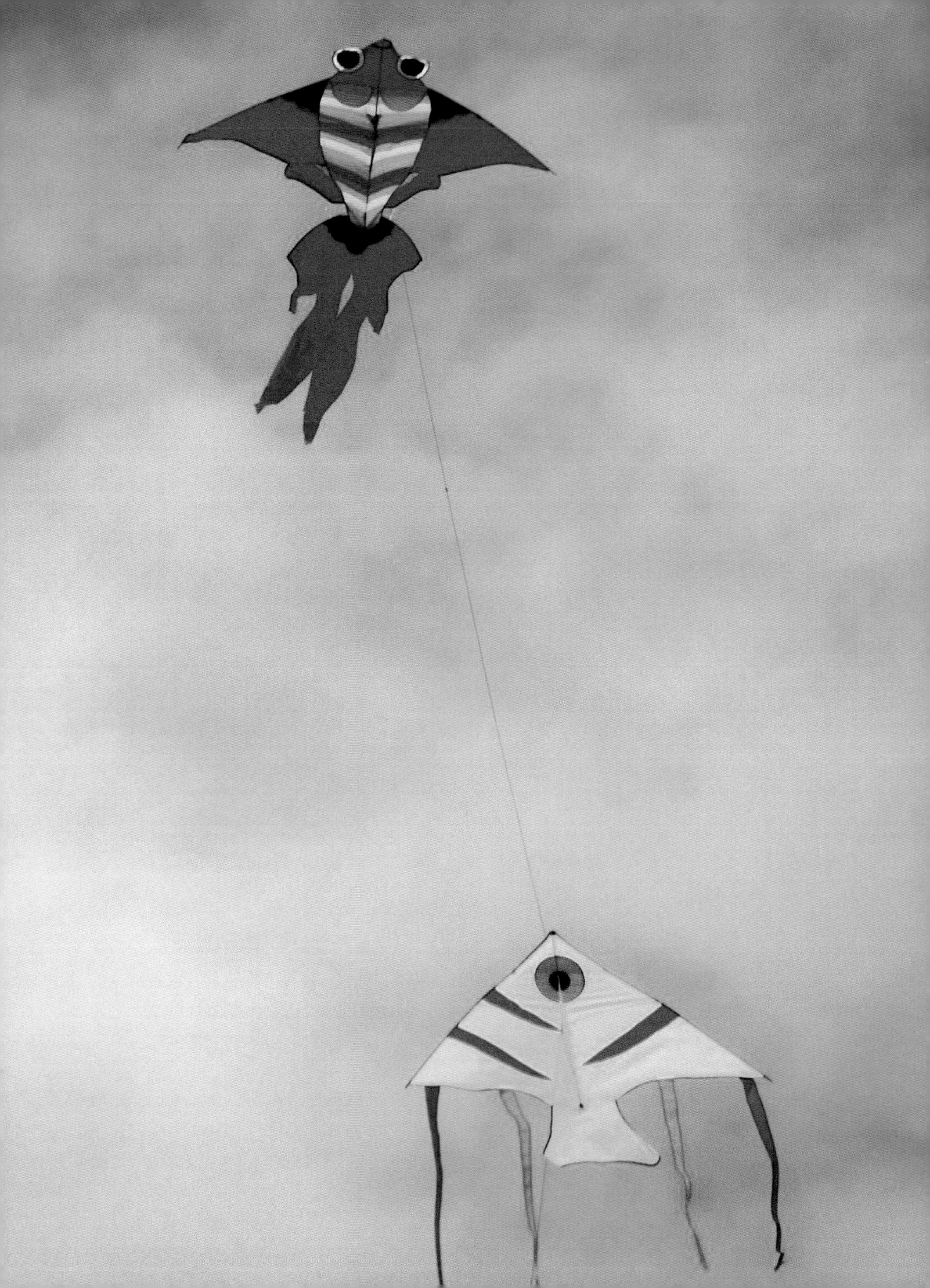

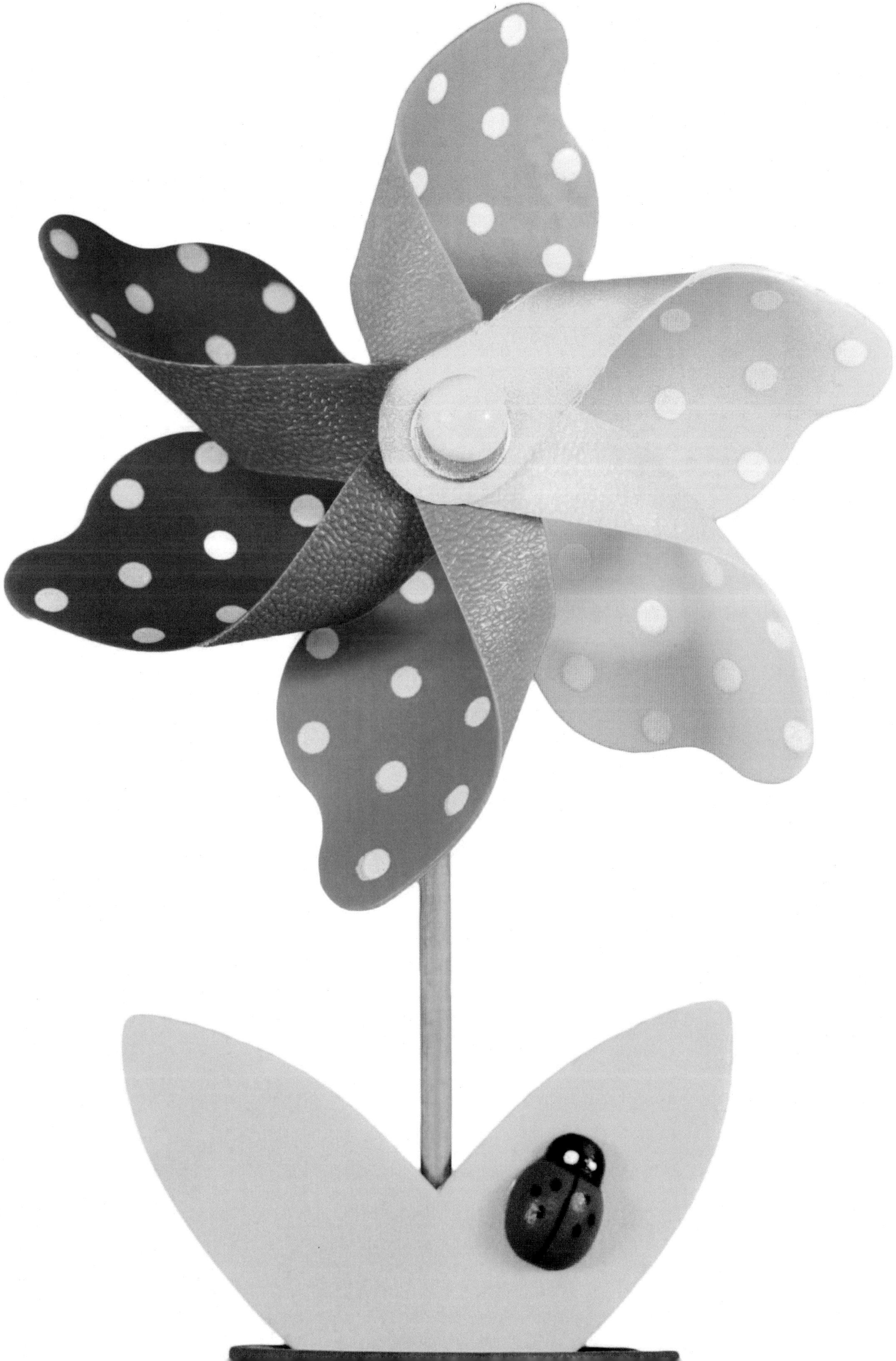

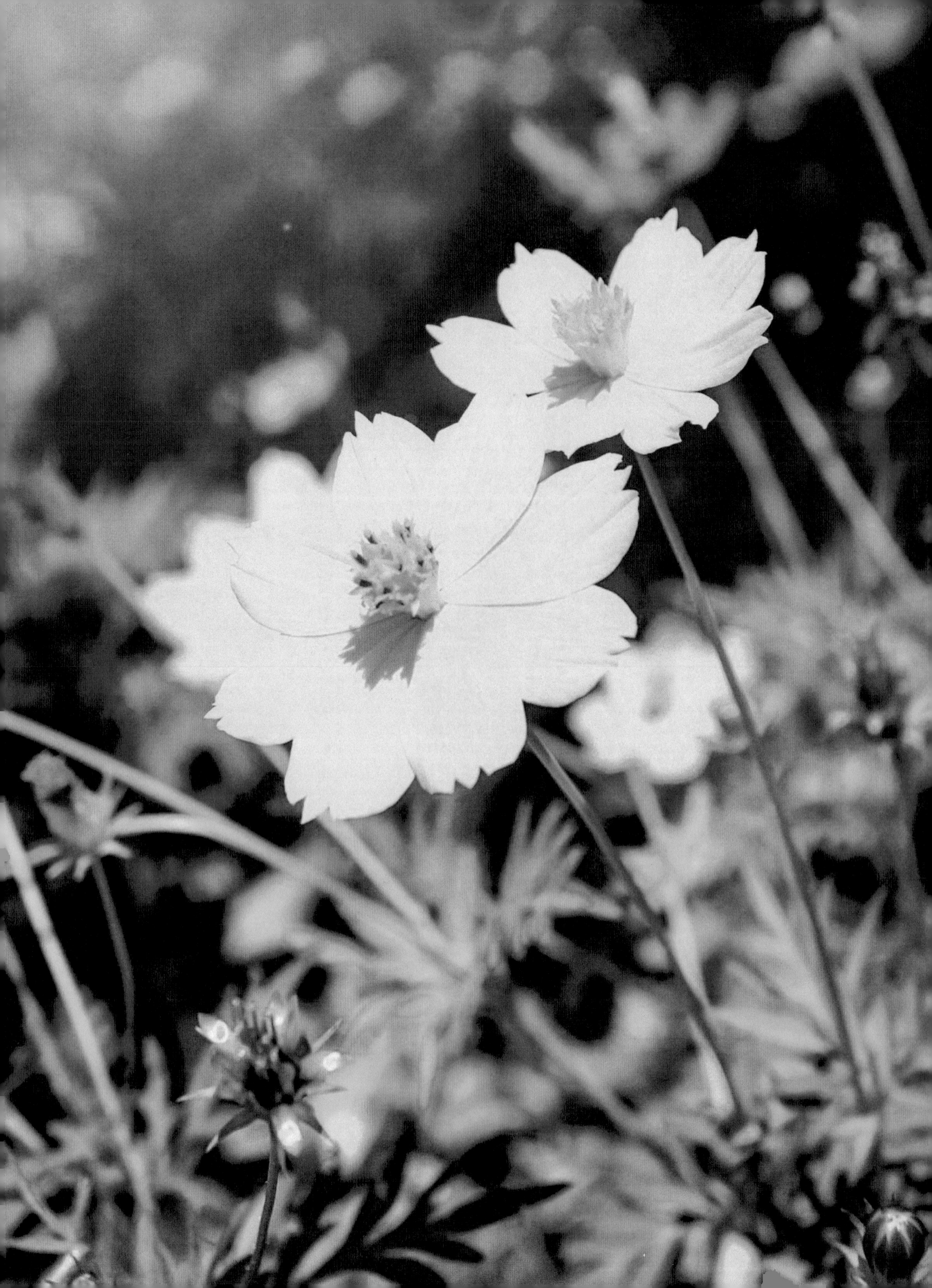

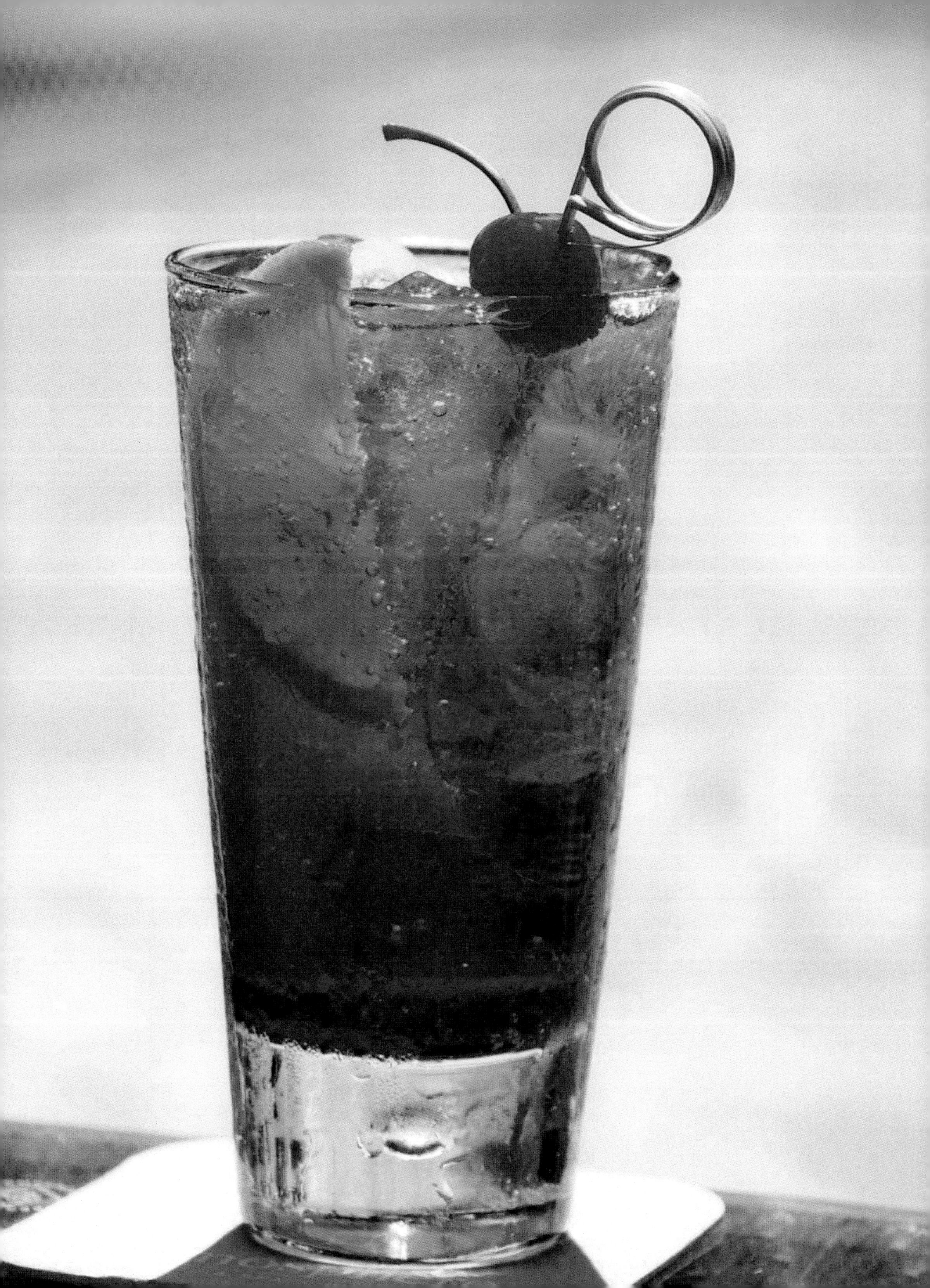

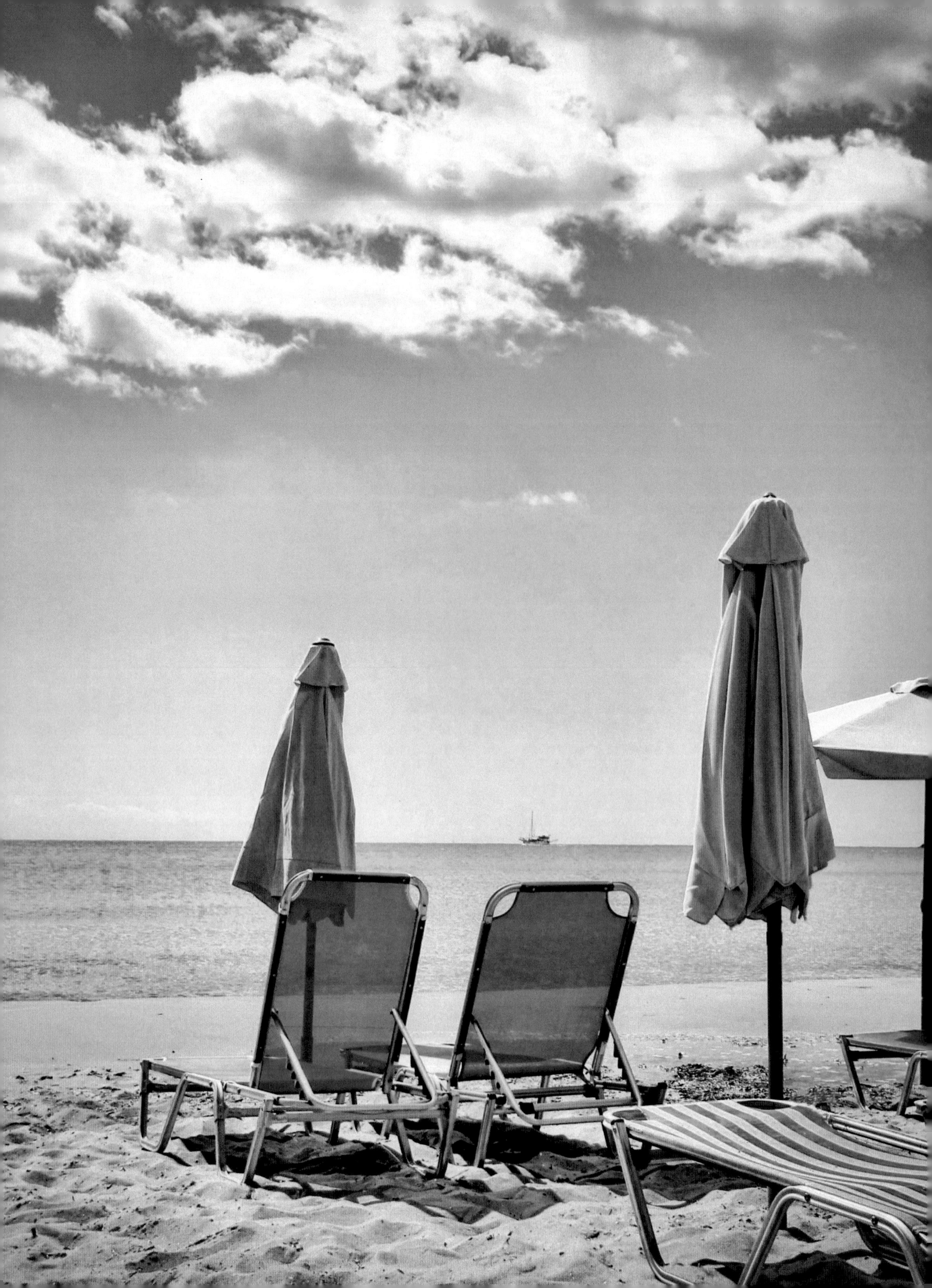

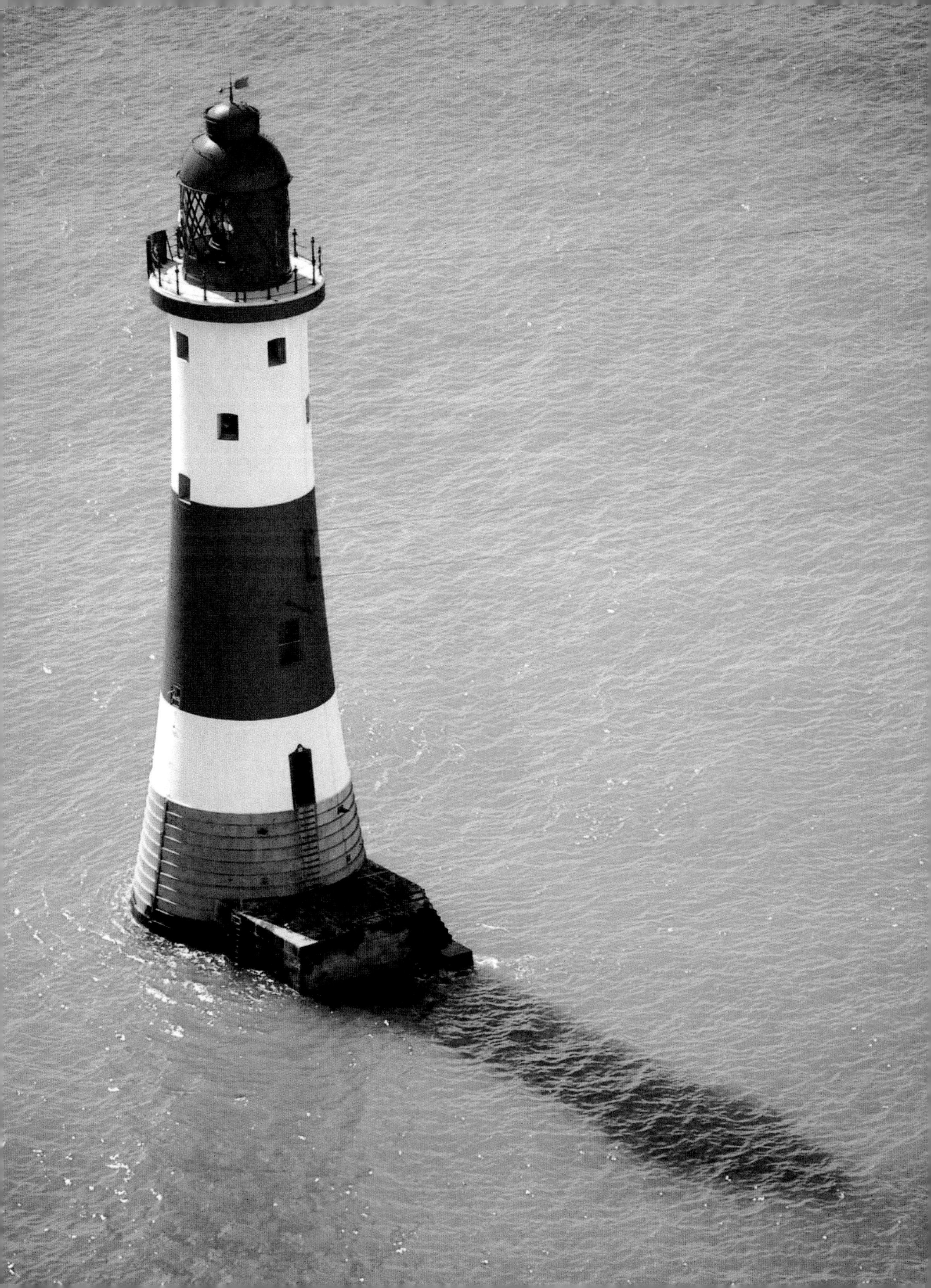

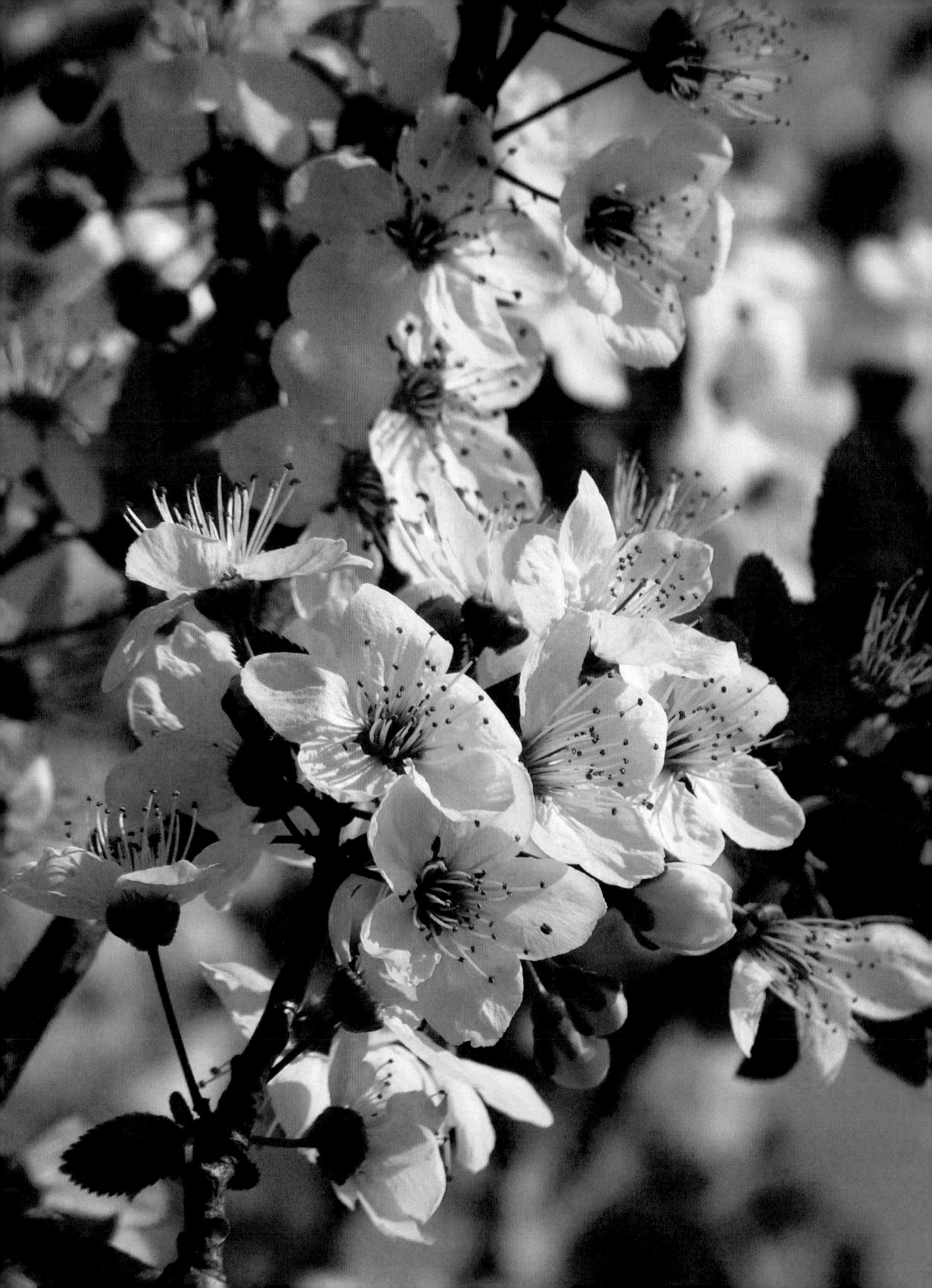

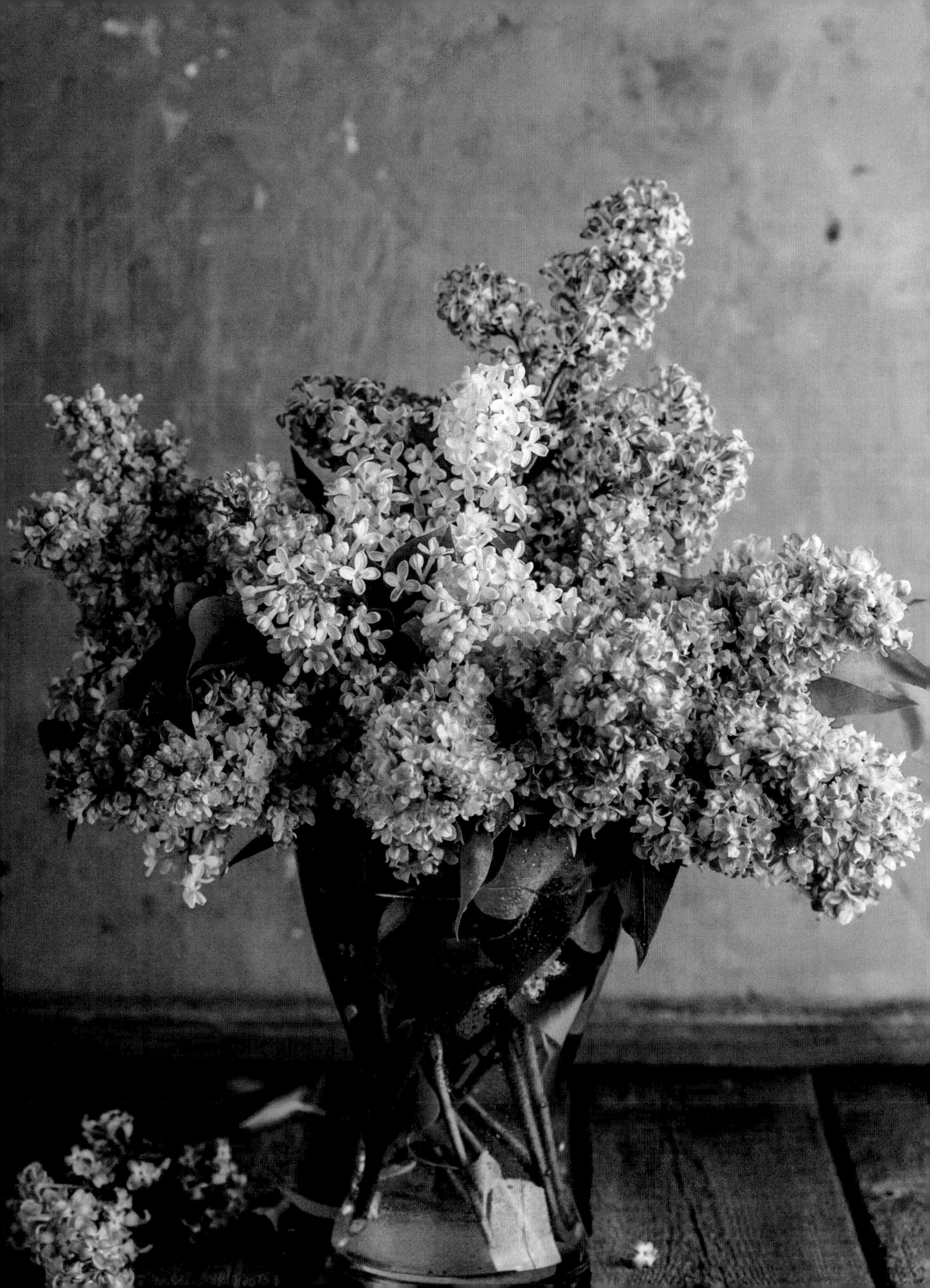

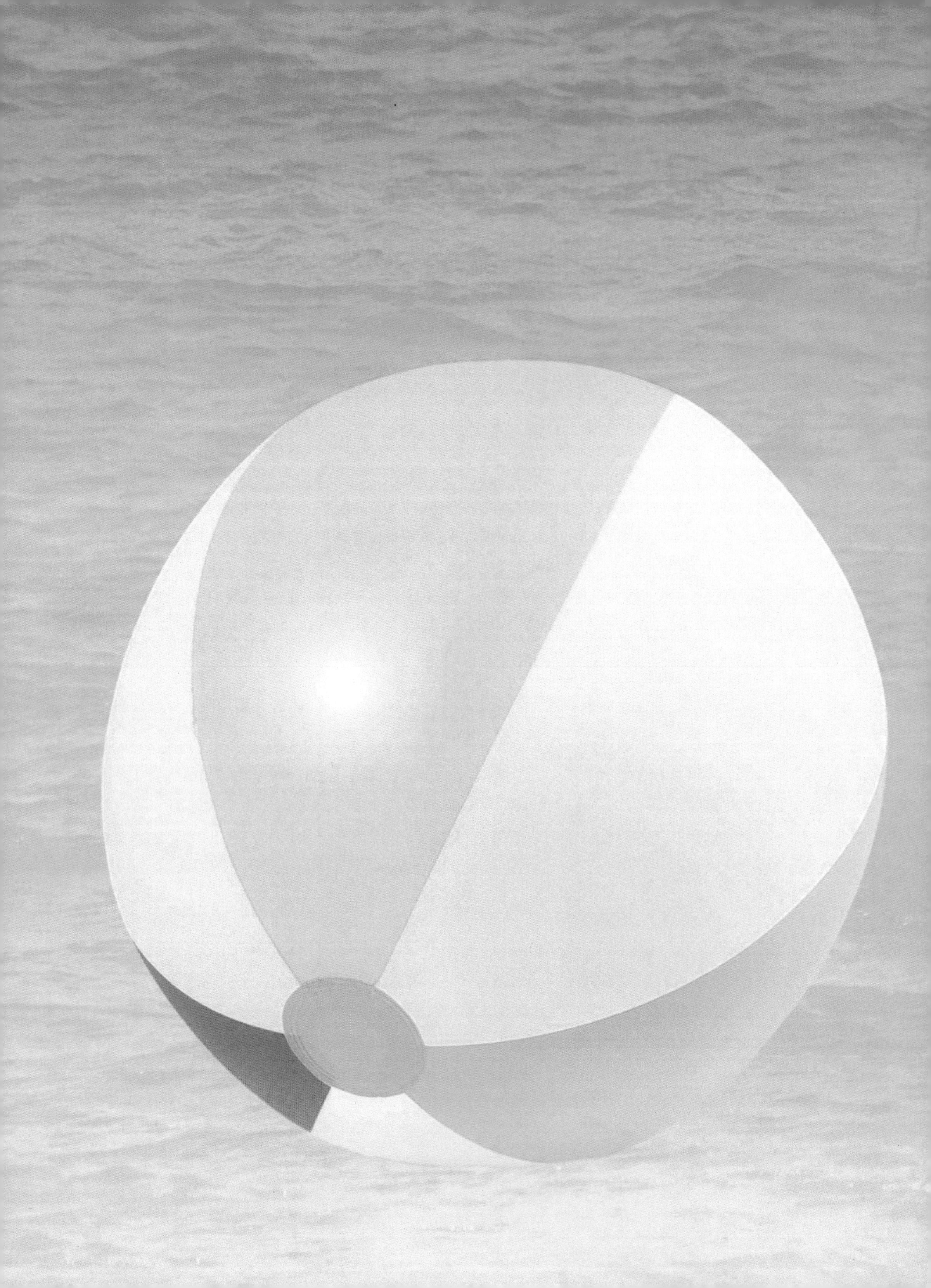

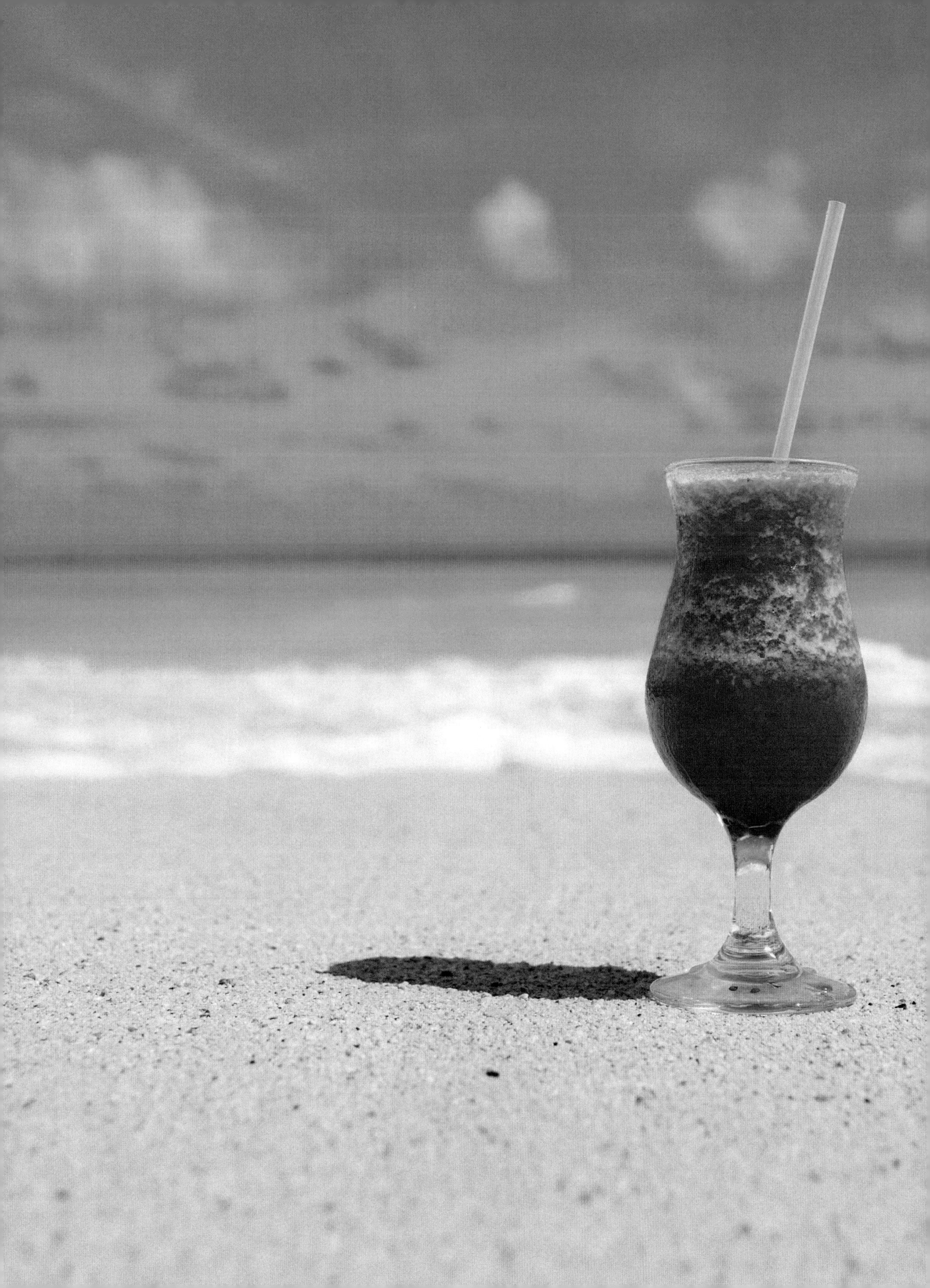

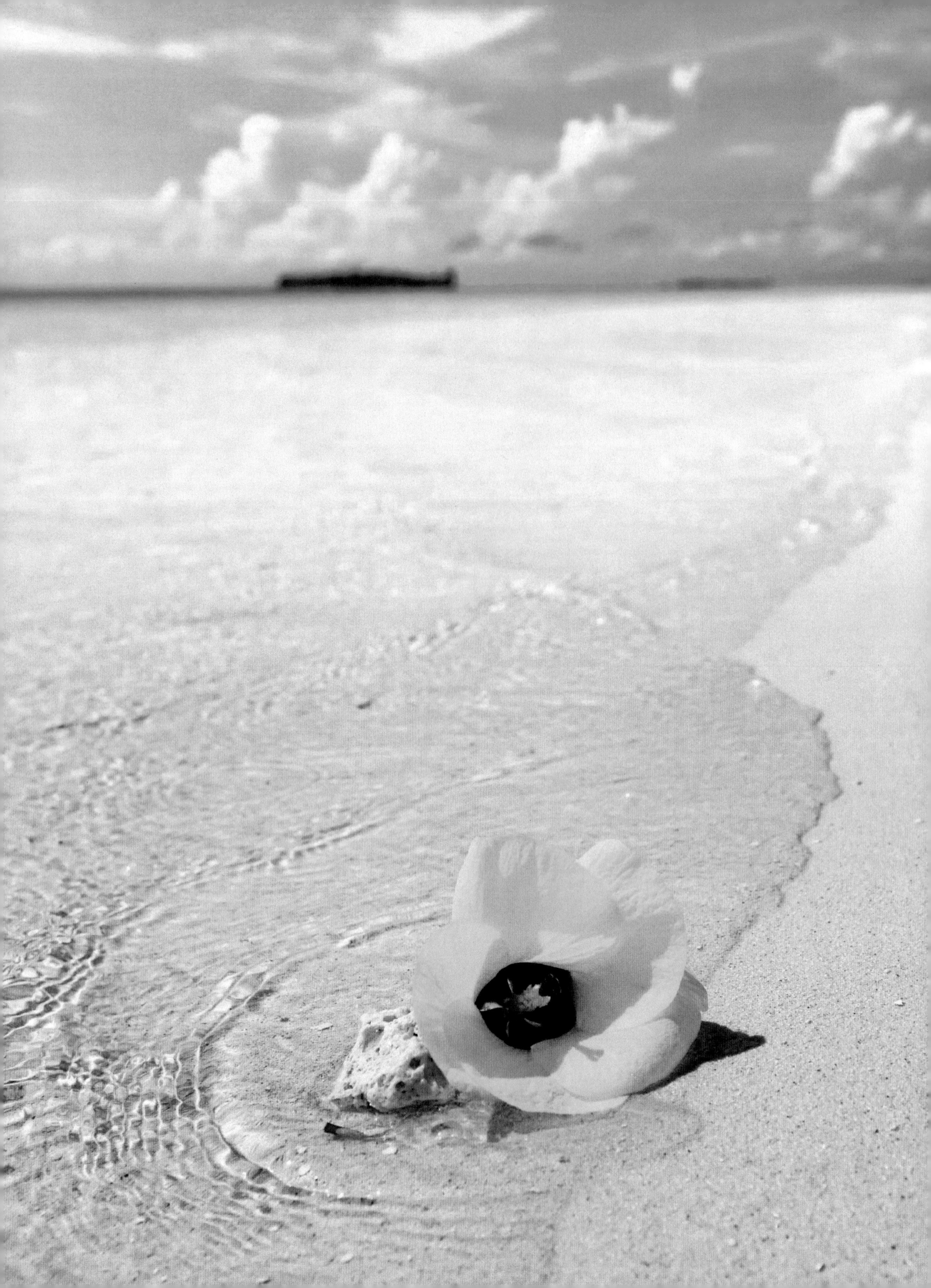

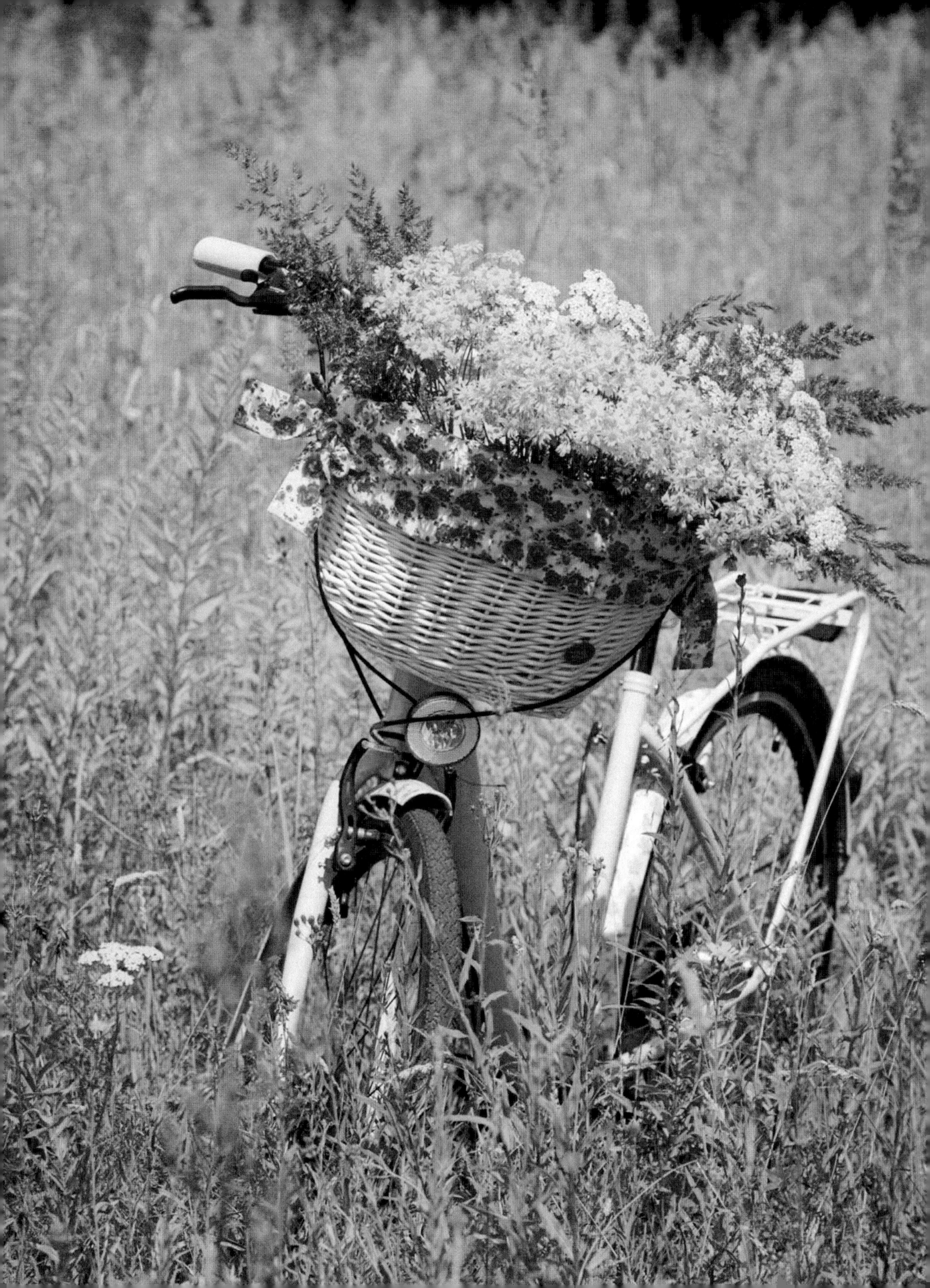

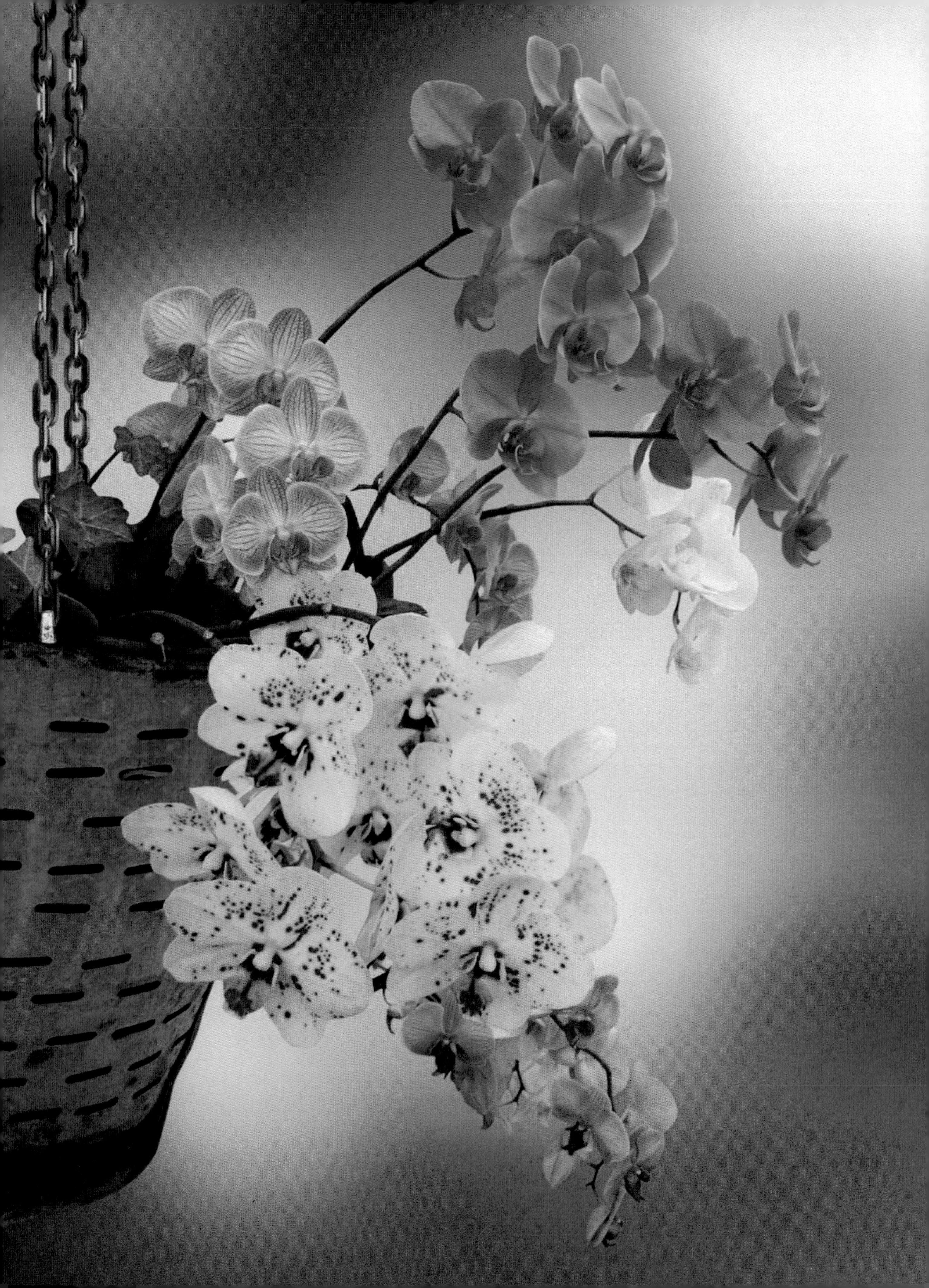

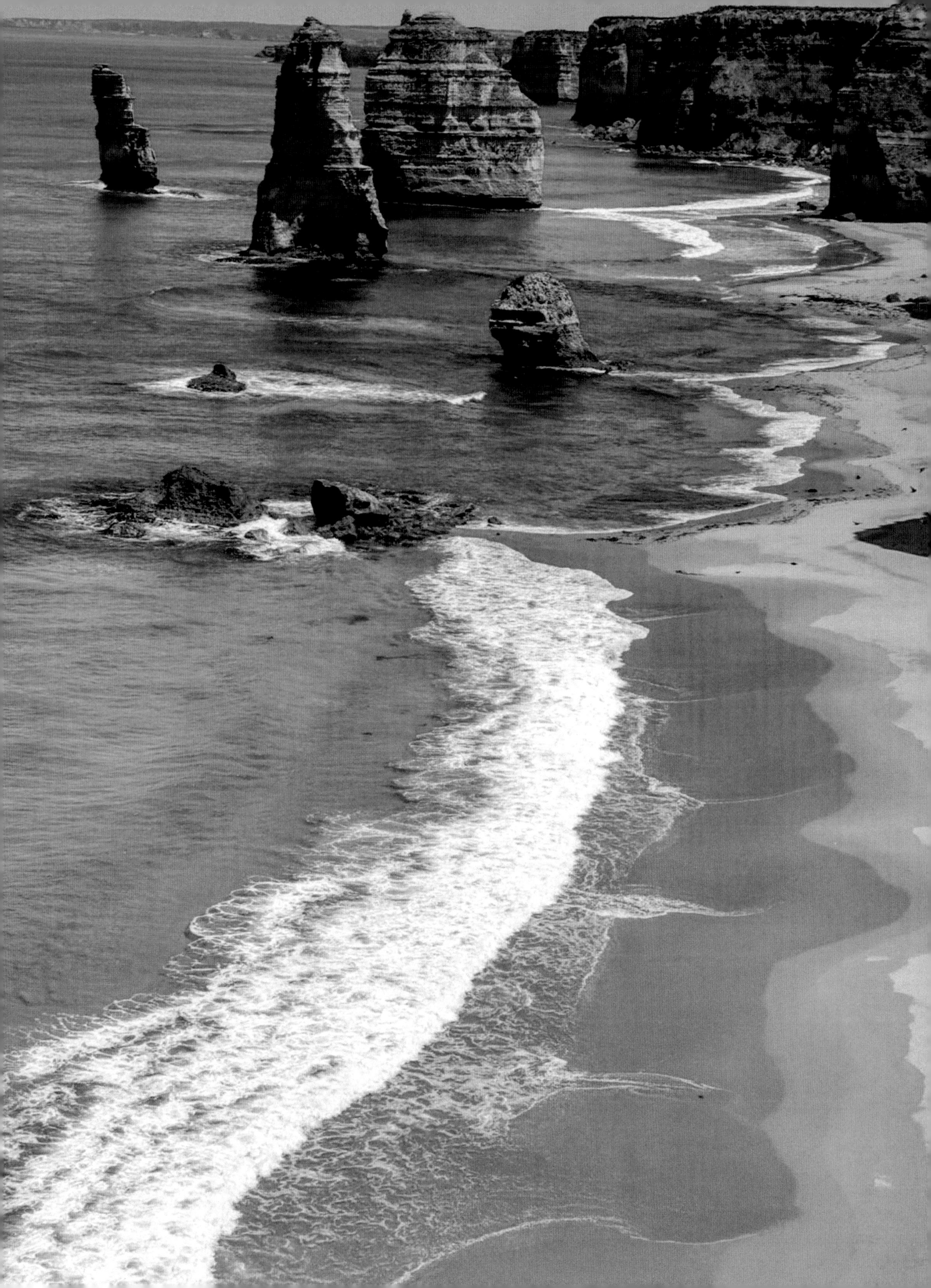

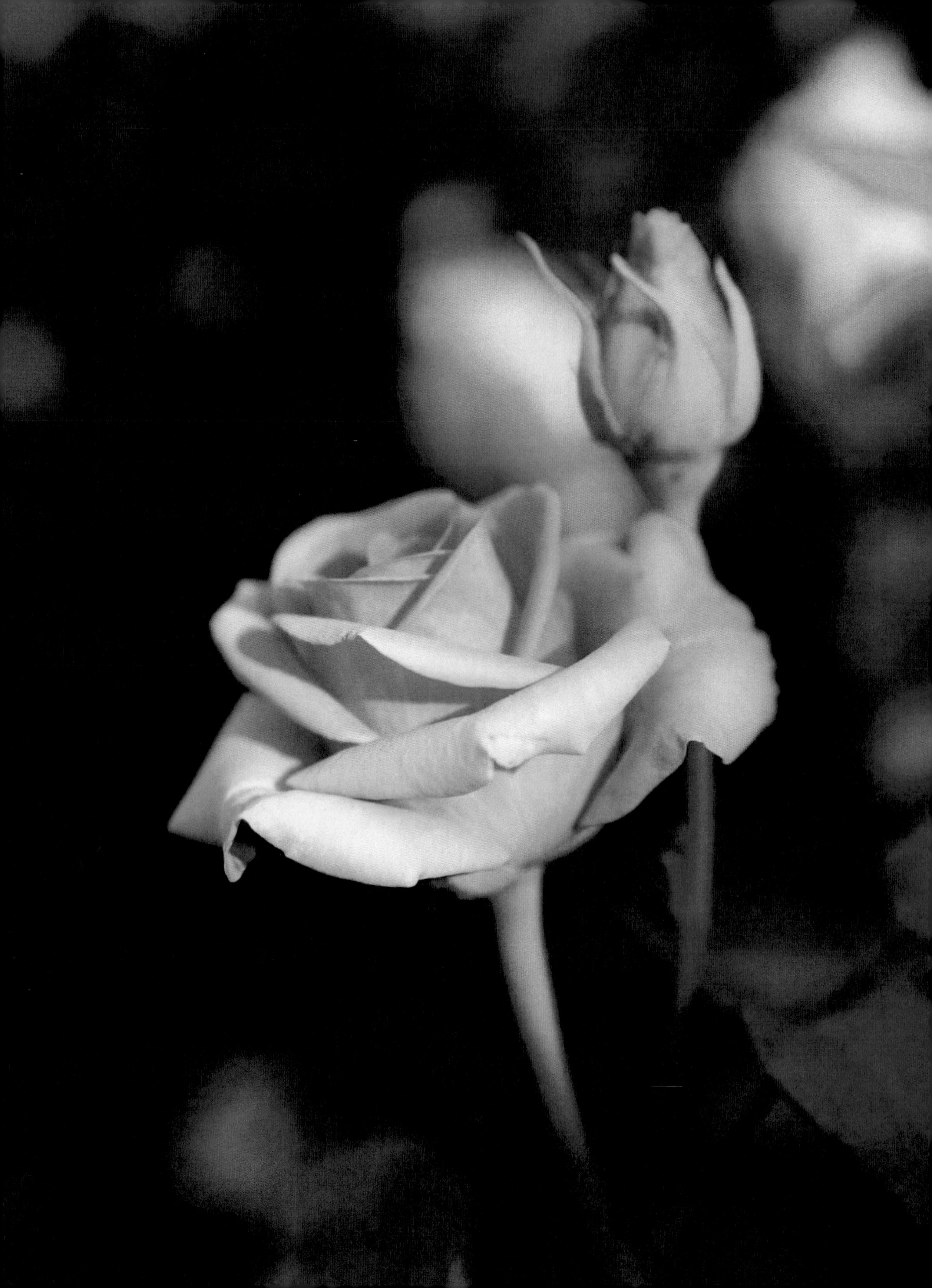

Made in the USA
Las Vegas, NV
04 September 2022

54686136R00026